T0342302

DAVID CAIRNS AND MARA CLEMENTE

THE IMMOBILITY TURN

Mobility, Migration and the COVID-19 Pandemic

BRISTOL
UNIVERSITY
PRESS

First published in Great Britain in 2023 by

Bristol University Press
University of Bristol
1–9 Old Park Hill
Bristol
BS2 8BB
UK
t: +44 (0)117 374 6645
e: bup-info@bristol.ac.uk

Details of international sales and distribution partners are available at
bristoluniversitypress.co.uk

British Library Cataloguing in Publication Data
A catalogue record for this book is available from the British Library

ISBN 978-1-5292-3005-5 hardcover
ISBN 978-1-5292-3006-2 ePub
ISBN 978-1-5292-3007-9 ePdf

Cover design: blu inc
Front cover image: Shutterstock/Asta Zaborskyte
Bristol University Press use environmentally responsible
print partners.
Printed in Great Britain by CPI Group (UK) Ltd,
Croydon, CR0 4YY

Contents

List of Figures

About the Authors

David Cairns is Principal Researcher at the Centre for Research and Studies in Sociology at ISCTE-University Institute of Lisbon, Portugal, working mainly in the fields of youth, mobility, education, employment and participation. He has participated in two large-scale European Commission–funded studies and is currently working on a project entitled 'Circulation of Science', looking at the development of scientific careers in Portugal.

Mara Clemente is Integrated Researcher at the Centre for Research and Studies in Sociology at ISCTE-University Institute of Lisbon, Portugal, and Associate Researcher of the Emigration Observatory in the institute. Her research interests focus on migration and gender issues, and qualitative research methods, with fields of expertise covering human trafficking, refugees, sex work and sex tourism.

ONE

COVID-19 and the Immobility Turn

The Immobility Turn is about transformations that have taken place in geographical mobility since the start of the COVID-19 pandemic, with long periods of restricted access to international and interregional circulation constituting a loss of the previously taken-for-granted freedom to travel. This extends to creating difficulties for industries that had grown reliant on free circulation of people – most prominently, tourism, universities and businesses employing large numbers of migrant labourers. Such is the scale of these transformations that there may have been a change in the pivotal position occupied by mobility in many societies, leading us to hypothesize that an 'immobility turn' has taken place. This follows on from the preceding 'mobility turn', which can be seen as a way of theorizing the multiplication of mobility in social, economic and political life, taking advantage of expanded levels of global interconnectedness.

Although the transformation in the fortunes of mobility is strongly associated with the pandemic, international travel had already attracted suspicion for other reasons, most notably the negative impact on the environment from aviation and the difficulty of hosting large numbers of incoming tourists in popular destinations. It might then be argued that the immobility turn is also a product of pre-pandemic issues, some of which we discuss in this book. Nevertheless, it was the rapid shutdown of societies and the curtailment of international travel in early 2020 that made many people aware of the fragility of free movement, creating the need to adopt more insular lifestyles. And while the turn towards immobility is not seen as a permanent change – although it may have felt so at times during the early months of the pandemic – the after-effects are likely to be long-lasting, creating an impetus for rethinking and re-examining some of the assumptions that informed the expansion of geographical mobility in the pre-pandemic years.

In this introductory chapter, we provide a brief outline of this position and an overview of what is to come in the book, starting with a look back at what was described as 'the mobility turn.' This was accompanied by the emergence of a 'new mobilities paradigm' that aimed to capture the sense of boundlessness that followed the multiplication of mobility at the end of the 20th century and beginning of the 21st century. The intention in the discussion that follows is to look at some key aspects of this expansion, taking into account not only rising levels of human circulation but also the diversification and apparent democratization of international travel, popularized to the point that regularly spending time abroad became a commonplace experience.

The mobility turn

The idea of an immobility turn is not entirely original and can in fact be seen as an extension, or modification, of prominent theoretical ideas expounded on in Chapter 2. For now, we can say that our approach to analysing immobility has conceptual roots from before the pandemic, and that we are entering a research field populated by many influential studies from various eminent scholars. More imaginatively, in addition to describing a literal multiplication in the number of people travelling within and between countries, the mobility turn also established a new vocabulary for social scientists; this was a discourse on mobility rebranded as 'mobilities' to reflect the expansionist outlook.

Although strongly associated with sociological theory of the 1990s, recognizing the societal importance of expanded mobility was not entirely new in itself, with mobility turn theorists drawing on pre-existing concepts, including the idea of a 'spatial turn', associated with the postmodern thinkers of the 1980s (see, for example, Soja, 1989). Going further back, the work of John Urry, discussed in greater depth in Chapter 2, also harked back to the urban sociology of Georg Simmel in the 19th century, including the idea of using mobility to enhance individualization processes, but also acknowledging the potential for generating social fragmentation (Urry, 2007, 20–6). We might, then, see the mobility turn as a means of describing a paradigmatic shift in the consumption of mobilities, defined by an expansionist orientation: more mobility and more problems with mobility, enabled by new developments in information technology, transport infrastructure and a greater reliance on aviation (Cresswell, 2011; see also Sheller and Urry, 2006).

In simpler terms, many people were able to become nomadic in their social lives and perhaps more global in their ways of thinking about the world, imagining themselves as interconnected and interdependent. But at the outset, we have to acknowledge that mobilities were a source of alienation as well as liberation. This ambivalence is reflected in the breaking down of the geographical integrity of careers and lifestyles, a growing sense of fluidity and lack of spatial fixity, enabled by the development of new modes of communication and faster, seemingly cheaper forms of international travel (Faist, 2013). While mobilities may have created additional possibilities for business and pleasure, the downsides included the degradation of the natural environment and the tension generated by the presence of millions of international travellers in the most popular destinations (Urry, 1995; Urry and Larsen, 2011). We can, then, acknowledge that there were societal problems during the mobility turn epoch, especially in regard to the sustainability of developments, and a lack of foresight that ultimately created difficulties for many travellers, ranging from tourists to labour migrants, and for residents in the places visited most often.

The COVID-19 pandemic as a turning point

Moving on from this position, in regard to the main hypothesis of this book, we believe that the COVID-19 pandemic represents a turning point for mobility – a shift away from open-ended multiplication and towards the subtraction of various travel possibilities from our lives, with this change becoming most evident during the first waves of COVID-19 and the abrupt stoppage of practically all forms of global circulation. While we are not arguing this change is permanent or irreversible – this is clearly not the case – it will be some considerable time before we can travel abroad in the same carefree manner as before. Additionally, even when most of us do decide that it is safe to take to the skies once more, there may be changes in the constitution of mobile and migrant populations, particularly if the economic cost of international travel rises and the range of accessible destinations contracts. This is not to mention the understandable reticence of people with mental and physical vulnerabilities to engage in non-essential travel, particularly when even the most rudimentary of sanitary protocols have been abandoned. In our own national context, Portugal, we observed that when full-scale tourism resumed in the spring of 2022, many travellers were from other European countries, especially France and Spain, rather than farther afield. Therefore, while it is important not to exaggerate the impact of the pandemic on mobility, we should not dismiss the long-term effects, especially as further impediments to resuming full-scale international travel emerge, including consequences arising from Vladimir Putin's invasion of Ukraine in February 2022.

More concretely, we can identify March 2020 – the start of the pandemic for most people in Europe – as the turning point for mobility, with a massive decrease in international passenger numbers and the raising of many barriers to internal and external circulation within and between countries. Less conspicuously, there has been a decline in the value attached to certain mobilities. This is something we reflect on in Chapter 4 in regard to the global circulation of higher education students, a practice that lost much of its lustre during the long periods of lockdown due to the loss of opportunities for engaging in culturally enriching social activities. International students obviously constitute a smaller population than international tourists, but the practice among students of moving abroad nevertheless represents an important rite of passage that had been lost. We might, then, say that alongside the hard-to-ignore quantitative changes, there are qualitative impacts arising from the immobility turn, and these issues are in need of investigation.

Research context

In regard to the academic context of this book, as noted previously, the study of spatial mobility grew massively in scale across the social sciences during the mobility turn era, most noticeably in geography, sociology and the interdisciplinary field of migration studies, particularly but not exclusively within the European context, encompassing work on 'softer' forms of circulation – moves abroad typically short in duration and often episodic or circuitous – in addition to the long-standing interest in migration and demographic change (King, 2002). This explains why the mobility research field now includes a wealth of studies on what can be referred to as classical forms of migration – people moving to a foreign country with a view to improving their economic situation and/or seeking some form of settlement – alongside work on less well defined modes of circulation – not only holidays but also education, work and training exchanges, with student mobility an especially popular topic (see, for example, Brooks and Waters, 2011; Feyen and Krzaklewska, 2013;

King and Raghuram, 2013). We therefore have a situation in which mobilities, and the representation of mobilities, diversified to reflect the expansion of international travel that was taking place, including recognition of the more fragmentary and piecemeal forms of migration wherein the dividing line between mobility and migration became blurred, with mobile individuals readily becoming migrants and vice versa.

Continuing a line of inquiry from previous publications (see, for example, Cairns, 2021a, 2021b), we have attempted to engage with this situation in this book, explaining why we discuss different and overlapping mobilities with a view to identifying contrasting and shared impacts arising from the immobility that has characterized the pandemic. In doing so, we focus mainly on three specific forms of mobility and migration. The most important, in terms of numbers participating, is international tourism, which somewhat ironically, and as discussed later in this book, is also one of the least understood by social scientists, with the problems generated by growing numbers of tourists downplayed due to the apparent economic benefits, making many social scientists reluctant to challenge the status quo. More popular, and less controversial as a research topic, is the study of the international circulation of tertiary education students, with a myriad of studies having focused on student migrants and others participating in short-duration exchange programmes like the European Commission-supported Erasmus scheme. Also acknowledged in this book is the ongoing importance of the more traditional forms of migration, including the practice of moving to another country with a view to entering its labour market. That we focus on these three mobility modalities in Chapters 3, 4 and 5, respectively, does not mean other forms of human circulation are less important, only that we feel that each of these examples provides us with an opportunity to look at different, and transversal, aspects of the immobility turn within our Portuguese research context.

The immobility turn in Portugal

Another important aspect of this book relates to the geographical context of our empirical research, which largely focuses on Portugal. With a population of just over 10 million people, according to the most recent national census, in 2021,[1] and a location on the western periphery of the European continent, this might seem to some readers like a slightly odd choice; why not opt for one of the core European Union (EU) countries or focus more directly on international comparative perspectives? The answer to this question is partly pragmatic, as we are both researchers based in Portugal's capital city, Lisbon, and we have made the study of Portuguese society a major part of our work and wish to build on our experience. Furthermore, during the pandemic, we, like most people, have been largely housebound, and this has limited the geographical scope of our work, especially in regard to international collaborations. From a more positive point of view, however, we can point out that Portugal provides multiple opportunities for studying different mobilities, including tourism, international student life and labour migration.

This is because Portugal is something of a 21st-century mobility success story, most visibly in its popularity as a destination for international tourists. As the statistics cited in the following section of this chapter demonstrate, the number of foreign arrivals increased massively in the decade prior to the pandemic. The same can be said about internationalized higher education, albeit on a much lesser scale. After a slow start, when relatively few students viewed Portugal as an academic destination, the country rapidly became a popular destination for learners from many different European countries and other global regions, including Africa, Asia and the Americas, as was the case in other Southern European countries in the pre-pandemic decade (Malet Calvo et al, 2020; Iorio, 2021). Less widely celebrated is the importance of Portugal as a destination for employment-seeking migrants. Historically, a relatively remote geographical position and fairly weak economic situation made Portugal a second-tier destination within Western Europe. However, in the years immediately preceding the pandemic, along with more job opportunities, the country offered foreign workers a relatively favourable reception compared to that in some other European societies (Azevedo et al, 2022; see also Peixoto et al, 2015). Nevertheless, while not generally problematized at a political level, labour migration to Portugal shares some of the same precarious characteristics found elsewhere, including problems with quality of housing for workers and issues in gaining full access to health and welfare services.

By considering three key forms of mobility in this book, we are to a certain extent looking at the immobility turn in Portugal at a transversal level, especially in regard to the parallel impact of events that unfolded during the first two years of the pandemic. However, while our analysis has a broad resonance, we do not make any claims towards representativeness in relation to characterizing Portugal, the EU or the wider global situation at this time, and our views obviously reflect our own opinions and experiences as researchers of various forms of human mobility.

The COVID-19 pandemic in Portugal

The timeline of the COVID-19 pandemic also warrants a brief note. Like most European countries, the first wave of infections arrived in Portugal during March 2020, and the spread of the virus has continued until the time of writing, over two years later. While COVID-19 may have been circulating, undetected, in Portugal before this time, the spring of 2020 marked the point at which society shut down, including the placing of multiple restrictions on the freedom to engage in internal and international travel.

This first wave of infections in Portugal, which lasted until May or June of 2020, was characterized by stringent sanitary measures, more so than in most other European countries. These included domestic confinement, the curtailment of interregional circulation and prohibitions on international travel. Following a relatively calm summer, a second wave of infections started in early autumn, again lasting several months, reaching a peak in October and November of 2020. This was followed by three further successive waves, the spread of the virus associated with a number of factors including the arrival of new variants, the ending of lockdowns and the hosting of several large-scale events without adequate safety provisions. For example, the third wave was linked to the decision to temporarily lift restrictions during Christmas 2020, a time when the virus was still widely circulating, and two football events, in Lisbon and Porto, respectively, contributed to the incubation of wave four in May 2021, an issue we return to in Chapter 6.

Wave five of the pandemic, associated with the milder omicron variant and coming after the fairly comprehensive rollout of a mass vaccination programme, was associated with fewer immediate fatalities, but there has been a greater cumulative impact due to this being longest wave in duration, having no definite end since omicron was basically 'allowed' to spread by the lifting of all the main sanitary precautions and the reopening of much international travel. The winter of 2021/22 was also the time during which much of our research was conducted, most of it between November and January, meaning that while we faced fewer legal restrictions, many risks remained and most people, including researchers, continued to conduct their work online even when this was no longer mandatory. The unstable epidemiological situation eventually provoked a sixth wave of infections during the late spring and early summer of 2022, when we were finalizing this book, the impact of which is uncertain.

Statistical background

A straightforward way of looking at the impact of the pandemic on mobilities is to examine available statistics. As already stated, the turning point in Portugal, and many other European countries, was during the early months of 2020. We can, then, talk about an immobility turn in quite a literal sense, in the form of lower numbers of people travelling, with the loss of international tourism being the most visible sign. Added to this is the loss of income from incoming tourists, with the pandemic starting in Portugal at a time when record levels of revenue were being generated from this source, at least according to the tourism industry's own statistics.

The expansion of international tourism

In locating our empirical research in Portugal, we are very well placed to study the expansion of international tourism: the country is popular as a destination for foreign and domestic visitors, and it experienced a period of unprecedented growth in international visitor numbers relatively recently, to the point where Portugal was alleged to have experienced a phenomenon referred to as 'overtourism' (Milano et al, 2019). The expansionist orientation can be seen in figures provided by the Organisation for Economic Co-operation and Development (OECD), which publishes data on a range of different tourism-related indicators, including the estimated expenditure of tourists while abroad and air and sea passenger numbers.[2]

Figure 1.1 and Figure 1.2 show that receipts from tourists rose in tandem with expansionism, suggesting a correlation between rising visitor numbers and profitability. It is also apparent that expansion ended at the start of the pandemic, with a dramatic fall in tourist expenditure and a sharp decline in the number of tourists making overnight stays in Portugal in 2020: a drop of over 50 per cent in total international receipts and a collapse in

Figure 1.1: International tourism receipts and tourist expenditure in Portugal, 2011–20 (Euros, millions)

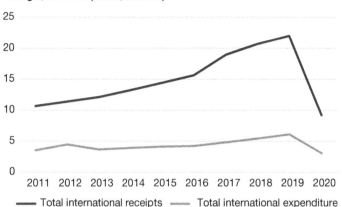

Note: 'Tourism receipts' refers to expenditure on inbound travel and goods and services while in the destination country; 'tourist expenditure' refers to consumption of goods and services while in the destination country.

Source: OECD, 'Receipts and expenditure', *OECD.Stat* [online], Available from: https://stats.oecd.org/Index.aspx?ThemeTreeId=10&DatasetCode=tour ism_rec_exp [accessed 10 April 2022]

visitor numbers from the pre–pandemic high of over 17 million overnight stays in 2019 to just over 4 million a year later.

In regard to the international picture, figures from the tourism industry provide some insight into what may have happened to visitor numbers in the first two years of the pandemic on a global basis. Data from the United Nations World Tourism Organization (UNWTO) for this period indicate the extent of lost business (see also Nhamo et al, 2020). The UNWTO Tourism Recovery Tracker compiles data on international travel, including air traffic, accommodation occupancy and COVID-19 restrictions, with a view to informing governments and tourism agencies of the current state of play.[3] The UNWTO's statistics indicate a quite catastrophic decline in the popularity of tourism, with a 97 per cent drop in the number of international tourists just weeks after the start of the

Figure 1.2: International arrivals and overnight visitors in Portugal, 2011–20 (number of participants)

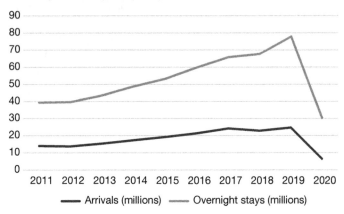

Source: UNWTO, 'International tourist arrivals', *UNWTO Tourism Recovery Tracker* [online], Available from: www.unwto.org/tourism-data/unwto-tourism-recovery-tracker [accessed 10 April 2022]

pandemic, in April 2020. This deep depression appears to have continued until April of the following year, when passenger numbers started to rise again, though never reaching even 50 per cent of the pre-pandemic peak. It is also notable that the recovery then faltered, coinciding with the spread of the highly transmissible omicron strain of the virus in autumn 2021.

From what we can infer, data from Portugal and elsewhere presents a quite bleak picture of the state of tourism at this time. We should, however, add that agencies such as the UNWTO have a stake in defending tourism, and it may suit the tourism industry's needs to create a 'bad' impression of their situation, especially when lobbying for state support. We therefore need to be circumspect about the industry's own claims, seeing their statistics as part of the marketing of tourism rather than as robust evidence that can be used by social scientists, a complicated and convoluted debate which we return to in Chapter 3.

Student mobility and migration during the pandemic

Another popular form of mobility, the international circulation of students, was also subject to massive disruption during the early months of the pandemic. This is a topic we engage with in Chapter 4, noting the generation of new economic pressures in Portuguese universities and the complications arising from the sudden switch to remote learning. For now, we can say that student mobility is another area in which the pre-pandemic years were marked by expansion in Portugal, as in many other European regions, with the growth of platforms like Erasmus and recognition within universities that fee-paying student migrants represented a very important revenue stream. This means that when the pandemic arrived, academic staff had to manage an enlarged international student population, and academic institutions faced the prospect of losing income from overseas enrolments should overseas students decide not to travel.

In regard to available statistics, unfortunately very little detailed information is available to the public – or researchers – about participation in Erasmus during the pandemic. We only know, from the European Commission's publicity materials, that in 2020, with a total budget of 3.8 billion euros, Erasmus+ supported around 126,900 organizations and funded in the region of 20,400 projects, which enabled almost 640,000 people to study, train or volunteer abroad.[4] Participation trends during the timeframe of the first Erasmus+ mandate (2014–20) also suggest incremental growth in Portugal, mirroring the pre-pandemic expansion found with tourism.

Figure 1.3 illustrates the apparent growth in the number of Erasmus students at Portuguese universities, although the figures for 'all participants' also include those participating in vocational training, work placements and voluntary work. That we witness no drop-off in 2020 is curious and suggests that what is being recorded is the number of enrolments made before the pandemic rather than the number of people who actually travelled, since

Figure 1.3: Participation in Erasmus+ in Portugal, 2014–20 (number of participants, thousands)

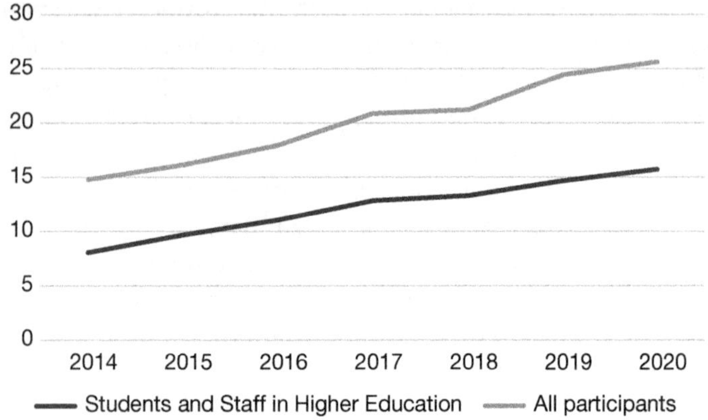

Source: European Commission, *Erasmus+ Annual Report 2020* [online], Available from: https://erasmus-plus.ec.europa.eu/resources-and-tools/statistics-and-fac tsheets [accessed 10 April 2022]

the likelihood is that many students either did not take up places or participated in online learning. It may also be the case that at the start of the pandemic, some students underestimated the severity of the crisis and travelled not realizing the risks they were going to encounter, although there would have been others who quickly returned home once it became clear that the pandemic was going to be a prolonged experience.

Our own research with incoming Erasmus students in Portugal during the first year of the pandemic, and contemporaneous studies elsewhere in Europe, makes note of these trends. This work also suggests that for those who did travel, there was a major decline in the quality of the internationalized learning experience during the initial lockdown, to the point where these students were unable to experience life in their host country to any meaningful extent, undermining the interculturality raison d'être of the mobility exercise (Cairns et al, 2021a, 2021b; Malet Calvo et al, 2021; see also Czerska-Shaw and Krzaklewska, 2021a).

Looking at longer-term student migration, where individuals moved abroad to study for at least a year, we also have limited data, but some data on pre-pandemic trends are interesting. The OECD publishes breakdowns of the percentage of international students enrolled in tertiary education institutions on a country-by-country basis. The most recently published figures relate to 2019, albeit with some data missing in regard to enrolments in OECD countries between 2010 and 2021. This means that we cannot yet assess the immediate impact of the pandemic on enrolments by overseas students for degree programmes, but we can identify signs of expansion.

As Figure 1.4 shows, in Portugal, the international student population grew significantly from a relatively low base of less than 3 percent of tertiary education enrolments in 2010 to almost 10 percent in 2019. As points of comparison, Figure 1.4 includes data relating to the country most traditionally associated with hosting overseas students, the United Kingdom (UK), as well as the OECD average. We can see that during this decade,

Figure 1.4: Enrolments of international students in tertiary education, 2010–19 (percentage of students)

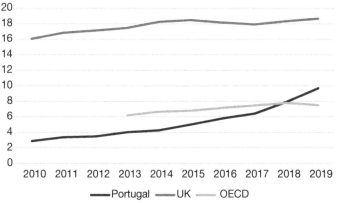

Source: OECD (2022), *Education at a Glance 2022* [online], Available from: www.oecd.org/education/education-at-a-glance/ [accessed 10 April 2022]

Portugal actually outstripped the UK in terms of growth and went from a position well below the international (that is, OECD) average to being slightly above it.

While statistics on the international picture are quite limited, figures from the Portuguese Director General of Statistics for Education and Science (Direção-geral de estatísticas da educação e ciência; see Figure 1.5) provide more insight into the national situation during the pandemic, with figures for both credit mobility, relating to short-duration stays (including Erasmus exchanges), and degree mobility for international student migrants at Portuguese universities; that is, students who moved for the entire duration of an undergraduate or postgraduate course.

Figure 1.5 provides an overview of trends in the period from 2015/16 to 2020/21 (different recording systems were used prior to this point). Unlike the OECD breakdowns, this presents a picture of what happened in the pre-pandemic

Figure 1.5: Credit mobility and degree mobility enrolments in Portuguese universities, 2015/16–2021/22

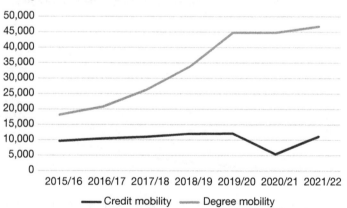

Source: Director General of Education and Science Statistics, 'Vagas e Inscritos (inclui inscritos em mobilidade internacional)' [Vacancies and enrollees (includes enrollees in international mobility)] [online], Available from: www.dgeec.mec.pt/ np4/EstatVagasInsc/ [accessed 10 April 2022]

decade and immediately after.[5] Looking at credit mobility, we can see fairly stable numbers of incoming students until the pandemic hits, when there is a dramatic collapse of almost 60 per cent. In contrast, degree mobility increased in popularity at this time. What is interesting to observe is that not only did degree mobility expand faster than credit mobility, becoming a much larger population of students, but it actually managed to thrive during the pandemic. This remarkable finding suggests a great deal of resilience on the part of student migrants, perhaps also reflecting the efforts that have been made by host universities at this time to both retain numbers and recruit more fee-paying students from abroad, a situation we explore further in Chapter 4.

Labour migration

Another form of mobility explored in this book is what we refer to as 'labour migration', meaning people who move abroad for employment purposes. In using this expression, we feel compelled to note some significant caveats and acknowledge our reservations about the classification of people as 'migrants'. We recognize that while this is a common descriptive category, it is far from being objective, politically neutral or innocent, and has in fact been used to legitimize restrictive migration and citizenship policies, producing new forms of exclusion and control following neocolonialist and neoliberal dynamics (see also Sharma, 2020), not to mention re-enforcing crude stereotypes. This ambivalence extends to migration statistics, the collation and interpretation of which are highly politicized, particularly in regard to the categories used as indicators of demographic shifts, which have the power to inform discourses that challenge social, political and economic hegemonies. Therefore, while some forms of migration, such as the attraction of fee-paying international students mentioned in the preceding section are seen as non-threatening, other practices, including labour migration, attract public and political controversy in some countries, although, historically, not in our Portuguese national context.

Bearing in mind this position, and the likelihood that we may be criticized for somehow appearing sympathetic towards people who have migrated for their own economic betterment, we still wish to consider the impact of the pandemic on this cohort. It is a valid aspiration for people to want to improve their personal and professional situations, and hence travel for 'the purpose of employment' (IOM, 2019, 123). This is an issue elaborated on in Chapter 5, but for now we can say that in some ways our orientation mirrors that of Portuguese society rather than the broader European or global norms, with terms like 'economic migrant', 'labour migration' and, especially, 'immigrant' pejorated to the point of becoming quasi-racist slurs and the temporary or permanent movement of racialized 'migrants' subject to intense scrutiny and articulated as '*problematic* mobility' (Anderson, 2017, 1532).

We nevertheless realize that other people do not share our views, and are aware of the use of 'migration' discourse to construct artificial difference and create exclusionary social hierarchies. We also know that a racialized approach to labour migration typifies the right-wing populist political forces that have come to dominate public discourse on migration in many countries in Europe and elsewhere, including Portugal to a certain extent. In less abstract terms, this discourse is also used to justify nation states' inability or unwillingness to guarantee decent work conditions and grant labour migrants access to public services, an issue we return to in Chapter 5. For now, we can say that there is irony in the fact that certain governments appear eager to spend huge amounts of taxpayers' money on creating the impression that they are stopping migration but are parsimonious when it comes to providing support to incoming workers, many of whom provide valuable and essential services in their host countries. It should also be noted that research and analysis of the migration experience and its impact on societies does recognize some benefits arising from labour migration, particularly in industries such as agriculture, not to mention the economic and social contribution labour migrants make to social protection systems, especially in societies that are demographically aging (see also Oliveira, 2021a).

We additionally note that the migrant population in Portugal has traditionally been quite small in terms of numbers arriving and settling. For example, the 'gross immigration rate', based on Eurostat figures and published by the official Pordata portal, suggests that in 2020, the permanent migrant population in Portugal stood at 6.5 per cent of the total population,[6] and the rate may be falling due to the pandemic limiting international travel. The most recent available data produced by the Portuguese Immigration and Border Service (Serviço de Estrangeiros e Fronteiras – SEF), as part of its characterization of migratory dynamics and processes in Portugal, suggests a decrease in labour migration from 2020 onwards, although variations are not easy to calculate. If we look at the resident foreign population statistics (described somewhat crudely as 'migratory stock'), we can see that there was an increase of 12.2 per cent in this cohort in 2020, but if we consider the number of new residence permits issued (referred to as 'migratory flow'), the upward trend of new permits was broken, with a decrease of 8.5 per cent compared to the previous year (SEF/GEPF, 2021).

The surface impression created by this data is that in quantitative terms, migration trends in Portugal have not been affected by the pandemic to the same extent as tourism. This does not mean that the migration experience has not become problematic, and this is why our approach in Chapter 5 is largely qualitative, looking at what happened to workers who continued to migrate, and circulate interregionally, at times when travel restrictions were in place and right-wing populism had started to be imported into the country, reminding us of the importance of the migration of ideas as well as of people.

Summary

This brief overview suggests that it is mobilities of shorter duration and perhaps those considered less essential that have been most affected by the pandemic. Many people stopped taking foreign holidays and fewer individuals took part in Erasmus exchanges, but others who had made significant investments in their education or were in need of work may have felt that moving abroad, or staying abroad if they had already travelled, was a risk worth taking. This implies that there are differentials within the immobility turn, perhaps oriented around the divide between non-essential and essential mobility, the latter persisting in a manner that the former could not. Whatever the long-term outcomes, we can say that the pandemic signalled the end of a sustained period of relatively untroubled expansion in various mobilities, although the trends emerging subsequently are far from uniform.

Reflecting on the opening remarks in this chapter and the quantitative trends discussed, the lack of understanding of the experiences underlying these figures has led us to realize that there is limited scope for making sense of the immobility turn through focusing only on statistical evidence and analysis of secondary materials. This is why the subsequent chapters of this book focus mainly on qualitative evidence. In doing so, we hope to add much needed depth and challenge some of the assumptions about mobility that arose before and during the pandemic.

TWO

Theorizing the Immobility Turn

In this chapter, we recognize the importance of prior scholarship on the meaning of the multiplication of mobility, sometimes rebranded as 'mobilities' (Urry, 2007). We note the importance of expansionism during the pre-pandemic era, especially but not exclusively in regard to tourism. From a positive point of view, expansion meant the diversification of international mobility, opening up new possibilities for personal gratification in the leisure sphere and, more instrumentally, widening the potential field of opportunities for education, training and employment. This implies that the shift towards mobilities was not entirely superficial, especially when there were possibilities for life-enriching social and cultural exchange to take place, echoing ideas from research on lifestyle migration (see, for example, Benson and O'Reilly, 2009, 2016). Less publicized was the negative impact made by mobilities on the natural environment, and the disruption to social life that could take place within host communities where visitor numbers had expanded to unmanageable levels (see also Urry and Larsen, 2011).

On this latter point, paraphrasing Oscar Wilde, we might say that there was a tendency for travellers to kill the thing they loved.[1] Tourism in particular had an unfortunate habit of homogenizing destinations, with the existing sense of place displaced by overcrowding and the erection of unsightly infrastructure – ugly new airports, carbuncle cruise ship terminals, noisy cafés and ghastly pop-up bars. The desire for expansion has nevertheless continued during the pandemic, albeit with a degree of adaptation. We have, for example, witnessed the emergence of hybrid travel experiences with remote working from different destinations growing in visibility, suggesting closer alignment between tourism and labour migration among the highly skilled.

Acknowledging the positive and negative aspects of the expansion of mobility, we argue in this chapter that in addition to higher levels of human circulation being economically and existentially important, there has been change in the consumption of mobility on which vested interests became dependent – an orientation viewed as desirable due to its apparent profitability. We might even say that approaches to mobility, and the defence of a global system of maximized levels of population exchange, came to represent an integral aspect of capitalist development, though one that also globalized risk and precarity. The pandemic threatened this position and created new vulnerabilities for travellers. Although the rapid spread of COVID-19 was not an intentional product of mobility expansionism, the virus was, literally, multiplied through the presence of millions of people in global transport networks, many of whom were engaged in various forms of non-essential travel to which they had developed an attachment. This can also be expressed in terms of sense of entitlement, with people paying for the privilege of travelling without restriction. The strength of this entitlement meant that when access to travel was restricted in order to help stop the spread of the virus, a temporary immobility imperative was created, changing the basic morality of mobility with a move away from it being seen as a harmless pleasure towards becoming a problem and something to be avoided. For this reason, it can be argued that the immobility turn was not just a sudden drop in the numbers of people circulating but also a shift in the value, and values, attached to various forms of spatial circulation, shifting the emphasis away from its positive aspects, including profit and pleasure, towards some of the more negative associations, including the spread of the virus itself. We might then say that there was a clash between the pre-pandemic economics-oriented expansionist values and the temporary requirement to be immobile, inviting a challenge from proponents of the former to question the legitimacy of the latter.

Return to the mobility turn

Before engaging with this debate, we return to ideas associated with the mobility turn, referring to developments in the decades prior to the pandemic. In fact, if we could return to 2019, we would find mobilities in full swing, and while reservations were noted about certain aspects of expansionism (for example, the 'overtourism' phenomenon we discuss in the next chapter), there were no real signs of the travel industry slowing down. On the contrary, we would have witnessed the development of more, and more intensive, forms of tourism; as the statistics cited in Chapter 1 highlight, the popularity of holidaying in our Portuguese research context was growing.

To make sense of this expansionism, we need to take note of the main social, political and economic imperatives that have made mobilities hard to let go of for many individuals and industries. Part of the 'problem' is fairly obvious. Mobilities have come to be seen as unproblematic aspects of social and economic life, and millions of people have grown deeply attached to travelling for work, study, training or leisure purposes, to visit family members and friends, or in search of a change of pace. At an individual level, such mobilities come to be perceived by some as essential to their lifestyles and livelihoods, but this does not mean that others will see them as vital. We can, however, say that leisure-oriented mobilities tend to be encouraged for economic reasons, particularly in terms of consumer expenditure. This explains why, in normal circumstances, this form of travel is regarded as politically unproblematic, especially as people are expected to return home once their economic resources have been expended.

There is also a kind of virtue attached to migration, especially the idea that people can move abroad to improve their financial situations and that migrants contribute to the economic standing of host societies. While this may be a somewhat romanticized view, it can also be said that without capitalism there would be no migration, and vice versa, at least not on the same scale (Messadra, 2001). Such perceived synergy means that labour migration is quite persistent and deemed essential to many people, to the point that they are able to evade censure, even during times of restricted circulation. It is only considered a problem when its meaning is politicized or related to securitization processes – although during the pandemic this situation has grown more complex due to public health considerations – and where societies are subject to pressures from nationalistic or xenophobic interests to keep groups seen as undesirable out of their national territories, even if this is economically illogical (see Carlà, 2022; Dalingwater et al, 2022; Erayman and Çağlar, 2022).

The mobilities approach

The mobilities approach is very much focused on forms of mobility that are non-migratory, with migration practices tending to be the preserve of demographers and economists. Mobilities then might be seen as an attempt to theorize what has been happening among mobility consumers and how the range of possibilities open to them has grown with the diversification of global interconnectedness facilitated by the emergence of new technology, more effective communications and faster transport links. The study of mobilities broadly reflects this focus, including studies from authors grouped together by the 'new mobilities paradigm' label, such as John Urry, Mimi Sheller, Peter Adey, Tim Cresswell and many others (see, for example, Adey, 2006; Cresswell, 2006; Sheller and Urry, 2006). The paradigm is both a reflection of mobility expansionism and a critique, with problematic aspects noted by authors such as Urry, who was in fact quite vocal in regard to the environmental impact of aviation in particular. Despite this warning, mobilities and global interconnectedness was generally seen as an opportunity to make oneself and the world more interesting through hybridizing identities and diversifying ways of spending money.

The pandemic obviously threatens mobilities by pathologizing non-essential travel and introducing rigid control to limit population circulation due to its role in facilitating the rapid spread of COVID-19 around the world, a point that mobilities scholars have been quick to note (Cresswell, 2020; Lin and Yeoh, 2020). The association international travel has with spreading and elongating the pandemic leads us to ponder why mobilities have remained so popular in the public imagination and seem to be returning even before the end of the public health emergency. The reasons relate to the resilience of the positive associations non-essential travel acquired during the period of expansion as well as the fact that during a pandemic there will be many people actively seeking respite from objectively miserable circumstances; we might describe this as a strange combination of nostalgia and escapism. Added to these reflections is the lack of completion of many people's mobility projects, including unfinished education, training or employment. Having bought into the idea that a kind of synergy is produced by the simple act of moving to another country, with the hope of unlocking processes of social mobility (Urry, 2000, 2), such travellers are going to be reluctant to change their plans, and the same can be said of institutions and industries with significant sunk costs and a dependency on income extracted from enlarged visitor numbers. Such thinking makes the continuation of various mobilities appear not only logical, both to consumers and stakeholders in the marketplace, but also near mandatory, even when to some people it still appears unwise to travel.

The end of the mobility turn?

These reflections take us to the turning point of the COVID-19 pandemic, and the prospect of a multiplication of risks posed to the traveller. When we talk about risks arising from COVID-19, we need to acknowledge the basic threat posed to physical and mental health by continuing to be mobile. Of course, it is important to state that international travel has always been potentially hazardous; there is the small chance that a plane will crash, a train will derail or a cruise ship will sink en route to the next destination. But aside from physical threats from both travel and the pandemic, more realistically, moving abroad will incur emotional and economic costs. Issues arise from the process of de-rooting oneself from one nation state and moving to another, including the generation of precarity. We made this discovery in our prior research, especially in regard to internationalized higher education, with students often paying handsomely for the privilege of studying abroad (see, for example, Cairns et al, 2018). Risks are also present for labour migrants, who may face racism and other forms of discrimination arising from restrictive policies and criminalization, a theme we return to in Chapter 5. In addition, for more-affluent travellers, there can also be a peculiar sense of dissociation from reality and losing one's place in the world.

We observed these phenomena in research conducted with international students during the first lockdown in Portugal: some faced the prospect of contemplating a return 'home' to places they no longer identified with, while others struggled to cope with the emotional consequences of being suddenly cut off from family members and other forms of financial support (Cairns et al, 2021a, 2021b; Malet Calvo et al, 2021). There is a risk that rather than becoming more connected with each other, people are internally disconnected by travel, experiencing disruption of their sense of self; or they may become socially cut off from old identities and networks in the attempt to forge new bonds. These are issues we return to in Chapter 4, but for now we can say that the human impact of internationalization needs to be acknowledged.

Liquid migration

Expanded mobilities also had major consequences for how travel was used during the life course. This included increased consumption, which may have had some benefits for travellers, particularly where economies of scale and heightened competition lowered some of the financial costs of tourism. Also, with more young people moving abroad for education and work, short stays abroad became a normal aspect of life for them; they travelled not just once or twice but intermittently, many times over a period of years or decades (Cairns and Clemente, 2021). Experiences such as these led to the establishment of a phenomenon that became commonplace in the decades prior to the pandemic, especially but not exclusively in the EU: the mass consumption of multiple forms of mobility across the life course, oriented around adventure and self-actualization rather than permanent settlement in a new society.

The people engaged in this practice might best be described as 'mobile subjects'. They are not 'migrants' in the traditional sense of the word, and will not think of themselves as such, but it is hard to ignore the fact that they have been spending substantial amounts of time living in other countries. It is the accumulation of experience that suggests a form of 'migration' is taking place, albeit disguised by this mobility being broken up and frequently interrupted, along with the maintenance of close ties with the home country. Such people have become migrants incrementally, and while there are no statistical indicators that adequately capture this phenomenon so that we might gauge its popularity, it is highly likely that this form of migration constituted another important aspect of the mobility turn, reflected in the European context by widespread use of expressions like 'free movement'.

Putting these reflections into more sociological language, this was a form of migration characterized by liquidity, with mobile subjects seeking to make their own migration trajectories using personal agency and resources, rather than basing their decisions on cost-benefit analysis or running away from existential threats and adverse economic circumstances (Engbersen and Snel, 2013; Engberson, 2018). This idea of migration as episodic and reversible mirrors broader theoretical recognition of the liquidity of social life, explored by authors such as Zygmunt Bauman (2000). Furthermore, this relates to not only the mobility decision-making of individuals but also broader political developments – most notably, the opening up of borders to enable greater numbers of people to move between countries on a temporary or circular basis (Favell, 2008, 705–6).

Although this phenomenon was seen as a positive development, especially in the EU, representing a kind of democratization of physical space, making migration intermittent also created many practical problems for those who engaged in it. There will obviously be emotional and economic costs arising from having to undertake successive dislocations, and people who 'fail' to settle in one place will lose out on many of the benefits that 'regular' citizens often enjoy, including access to free or affordable health and welfare services. We might, then, say that the 'liquid migrant' lacks the literal grounding in place that is offered by traditional migration processes, with the spectre of precarity emerging from the broken-up nature of the liquid migration experience, not to mention the lack of any 'real' connection to the places being visited. Such fragmented lives might not then be as desirable as we might think, particularly when people come to realize that certainty, and security, are not necessarily bad things.

The logic of immobility

The unsettling nature of the pandemic compelled us, practically overnight, to question the need for so many different forms of non-essential mobility. This is not only due to the epidemiological risks that were being generated, but also because of a degradation in the capacity of international travel to make a meaningful contribution to our sense of self-worth. Previously, the detrimental aspects of travel were relatively easy to set aside, since there was rarely any immediate risk. Most travellers had no real qualms about the impact of aviation on the environment, perhaps thinking that a token financial contribution to an airline could compensate for their increased carbon footprint. But when there is an actual risk to one's health in the form of a potentially deadly virus, it becomes logical to be immobile. However, once the first wave of the crisis had passed, some people continued to travel even though COVID-19 infection rates were extremely high, suggesting that they had scant regard for their own health or the well-being of fellow travellers.

People who engaged in non-essential travel during the pandemic can obviously be seen as selfish idiots, but there is a need to understand, in less pejorative terms, why people would want to travel when it is logical not to do so. They may have simply decided that it was a risk worth taking, or the temptation was too hard to resist and the potential rewards too great, particularly if already habituated to a certain amount of disruption. As mobility researchers, we are aware of the fact that people enjoy the experiential aspect of international travel. Travelling is already quite arduous and uncomfortable, and while existing problems might have intensified during the period when sanitary measures were being enforced, the experience did not become unsufferable. The heightened personal gain of surviving the endurance test may have even helped to offset any potential qualms.

We might also take note that not everyone was against travelling, and there may have even been encouragement. The apparently transgressive behaviour of travelling during lockdown was in fact quite easy to overlook, especially when there was tacit endorsement from the aviation industry, concerned no doubt with its own economic survival. This latter point can be extended to businesses in societies like Portugal that are dependent on tourism, and where there have been genuine concerns about the impact of the pandemic on the economy, especially in the hospitality sector. More significantly, the introduction of testing and vaccinations gave people a literal pass. As such, with the exception of the first wave of the virus, it was still possible to travel, despite some practical obstacles, with the qualification of meeting entry requirements relating to negative COVID-19 test results and/or appropriate vaccination status.

Moral economy

This does not, of course, mean that travelling was taking place entirely without any sanctions whatsoever. While the legal restriction of mobility seems to have been somewhat lax, or at least became fairly easy to circumvent, we cannot necessarily say the same about how pandemic-era travelling was received socially. While those undertaking non-essential voyages may have viewed their own actions as valid, this was not necessarily the view among people who were put at risk by the unwillingness of others to stay at home. This may in fact have led to a kind of COVID-19 'tourist gaze' (Urry and Larsen, 2011), with the presence of outsiders generating consternation – especially when visiting people who had less freedom to circulate – to the point of being seen as a form of imperialism akin to the 'medical gaze' hypothesized by Foucault (Korstanje and George, 2021, 79). This suggests a shift in the moral meaning of mobility that, while neither permanent or absolute, questioned the value of international travel for individuals and for societies. While much mobility is already morally suspect due the negative impact on the environment, the immediate and visible aspects of the pandemic were more effective in morally problematizing international travel.

At a quotidian level, travel has always involved weighing up costs and benefits, although perhaps without the prospect of suffering a self-inflicted ethical injury. The position changes when international travel is effectively outlawed, making it easier for people to morally damage themselves. A related issue concerns the circumnavigation of ethical strictures, including attempts by travel-dependent industries to remove legal restrictions as soon as possible, irrespective of the actual epidemiological situation. We can then see that there is common ground between determined travellers and certain parties in travel-dependent industries in that both want the same outcome: a return to the skies as soon as possible, irrespective of the societal consequences.

To help explain how this particular scenario might work, we can draw on the idea of 'moral economy' popularized by the Marxist historian E.P. Thompson in *The Making of the English Working Class* (1963) and developed further in 'The moral economy of the English crowd in the eighteenth century' (1971).[2] In addition to acting as historical accounts of civil unrest at the time, these influential works demonstrate how an economically oppressed class can generate its own moral values in reaction to social and economic conditions that are perceived as unjust. This involves forging cross-class alliances, even between groups who are diametrically opposed in their social and economic positions. The English peasantry could, then, align with landowners and influence government policy, since they had a shared interest in opposing the government of the day. Updating the principle, we can say that travel industries were able to ally themselves with frustrated travellers to defeat the authority of the state, which had temporarily ceded responsibility for public policy to medical science. This apparent rebellion becomes stronger as sufficient numbers of people feel systematically deprived of a resource they see as economically and ontologically vital – namely, access to international travel. The oppressed alliance sees its protest actions as virtuous, according to its own self-generated moral position – essentially creating a victim narrative – which is re-enforced through appeals to the authority governments ordinarily obey – namely, market forces. Policymakers and experts, especially those with responsibility for public health, are given the unenviable task of trying to make decisions that cannot please everyone and which may result in themselves becoming targets for opprobrium from the protesters, thus furthering the cycle of moral indignation and victimhood.

By adopting a moral economy perspective in regard to pandemic-era travel, we are now able to explain the apparent perversity of policymaking in relation to the abrupt lifting of restrictions on travel, an issue that we return to later in this book. For now, we can say that the approach was obviously successful, and as we move into the third year of the pandemic, international travel has largely reopened without any serious efforts being made to limit the spread of the virus. In fact, such was the rapidity of the policy reverse, airports were not adequately equipped to manage the sudden return to expanded visitor numbers. This inevitably created a huge mess with overcrowding and cancelled flights, although the mobile subjects had, arguably, no one to blame but themselves.

Summary

As we move forward in this book, we look at some concrete examples relating to the clash of values hypothesized in this chapter. Significantly, we are able to update the moral economy perspective to reflect the norms and values of a mobility-oriented consumer society. In its classical orientation, 'moral economy' was used to denote what was essentially a class struggle and alliances of different interest groups; now, certain vested interests – including members of the public aligned with economically important industries – are able to exercise their entitlements to international travel even when there may be negative consequences, including a potential prolongation of the disruption to mobility, the very thing that they are protesting against.

Reflecting on the discussion in this chapter, a significant amount of work clearly needs to be undertaken before societies can safely return to peak levels of visitor numbers, suggesting that wisdom has been lacking among those who want to travel again. Tourism in particular needs to prepare for the reactivation of its travel routes and recognize that many people remain anxious about the apparent lack of care being taken, furthering their travel reticence. From a long-term perspective, travellers might also want to take more notice of the problems their presence generates, particularly in regard to the problematic societal impact of their activities when practised to excess, a theme we return to in the next chapter.

THREE

From Overtourism to Undertourism, and Back Again

In this chapter, we explore the impact of the COVID-19 pandemic on the tourism industry in Portugal, using findings from fieldwork conducted during 2021 and 2022. The aim is to learn more about the challenges industry stakeholders have faced during an unprecedented and unpredictable public health emergency. In Chapter 1, we noted the extent of the financial losses incurred during the first two years of the pandemic, and in Chapter 2, some of the moral quandaries that arose out of attempts to keep travelling during times of restricted circulation. We now wish to take a more in-depth look at these issues.

In order to do this, we have adopted a number of pre-existing theoretical concepts. The first is a relatively familiar theme: the idea of overtourism. This is a topic that attracted a large amount of academic scrutiny during the decade of expansionism that preceded the pandemic (see, for example, Capocchi et al, 2019; Milano et al, 2019; Volo, 2020), becoming a cause celebre in many of the cities that were most visited by international tourists. This includes Lisbon and Porto in Portugal – and elsewhere, Amsterdam, Barcelona and Venice – where in the years prior to the pandemic, tourist numbers increased massively (Malet Calvo and Ramos, 2018). As well as revisiting the concept of overtourism, we try to make sense of the sudden collapse in tourist numbers during the public health crisis. While in Chapter 1, we discussed this transformation using statistics on lower visitor numbers and lost revenue, we now wish to appreciate changes in the meaning of international tourism using the idea of 'undertourism'. While this is another pre-existing concept, having been used in the past by tourism researchers to help identify new sites for exploitation (Gaitree Gowreesunkar and Vo Thanh, 2020), we interpret undertourism somewhat differently, as a term that describes issues arising from the sudden decline in visitor numbers within a previously popular destination.

Tourism in Portugal

Before we address these theoretical issues, we want to provide a brief commentary on the significance of tourism in Portuguese society. While most countries attract visitors who make a contribution to the national economy, in Portugal the tourism industry occupies a prominent place in public and political discourse, with the country's status as a popular destination for people from across the world seen as a source of civic pride. The industry itself is keen to stress its economic importance, with success advertised in terms of rises in visitor numbers and their estimated expenditure, issues we introduced in Chapter 1. More recently, there has also been recognition of the tourism industry's contribution to reaching sustainability goals, thereby addressing the potential negative impact made by international travel on the environment.[1]

The importance of tourism in Portugal helps explain why the downturn in the industry's fortunes at the start of the pandemic was such a huge concern, marking as it did the end of a long period of success in a country that as recently as a decade ago was embroiled in a major economic crisis (Fletcher, 2011; Fletcher and Neves, 2012). This may help explain why the plight of the tourism industry and associated sectors of the economy, including aviation and hospitality, featured prominently on news reportage in Portugal since the very first days of the COVID-19 crisis, with the sight of grounded planes, empty airports and cordoned-off beaches becoming some of the most iconic images of the initial year of the pandemic. International tourism obviously matters a great deal, and we should also note that the significance of tourism in a destination country like Portugal is different to its significance in countries that are more likely to be sending people abroad. In those countries, the loss of tourism is associated with the removal of freedom to engage in unrestricted travel, but in destination countries the internal narrative is going to be somewhat different, focused on the loss of incoming tourists and their money rather than the loss of entitlement to be international tourists.

Before we continue, we should add a further brief note about how the status of tourism in Portugal has acted as a kind of barometer of the evolution of the COVID-19 crisis in the national context. The impact of the virus was measured not only by numbers of infections, hospital stays and fatalities, but also according to the severity of restrictions imposed on international travel, such as legal requirements for vaccine certificates, negative lateral flow tests and quarantine after returning home. We might say that the more restrictions in place and the fewer the number of travellers, the worse the pandemic was assumed to be. This approach also meant that the lifting of restrictions was interpreted as a sign that the pandemic was in remission, irrespective of the actual epidemiological situation. As we explored in the previous chapter, this is a reflection of the industry's political strength and its ability to leverage the support of determined travellers via the use of moral economy arguments against the government and public health experts. This strategy arguably led to the premature end of most sanitary measures and the opening of full-scale tourism, possibly contributing to the start of a sixth wave of infections in spring 2022.

Overtourism and undertourism

To help us move forward, we want to look at two similar-sounding but contrasting ideas that help explain how tourism expanded in the decade preceding the pandemic and contracted after the start of the crisis. Having presented some fairly simple statistics suggesting a drastic change in international tourism's popularity in the early months of the pandemic (see Chapter 1), we now want to consider why this has been such a problem for the tourism industry and, by association, societies like Portugal that have become dependent on incoming visitors. In addition to highlighting some of the fairly self-evident problems that have arisen, such as loss of revenue, we look at the opportunities created by the presence of fewer travellers, including engagement with what are defined as models of sustainable tourism.

Overtourism

Overtourism is an issue many of us should be familiar with by now, whether as a visitor to an overcrowded destination or a resident of such a place. In descriptive terms, it is fairly easy to say why overtourism happens: too many people want to visit the same place at the same time, attracted by its natural beauty, historical significance or iconic appearances in films and television programmes. Tourism then becomes a problem as the expanded numbers cannot be adequately hosted, ruining the visitor experience and creating tensions within local communities. In terms of what overtourism looks like, common signs include the presence of oversized cruise ships on city riverbanks, industrial-scale short-term letting in residential areas and multiple low-cost airlines competing for business at busy airports, with the widespread use of information technology having been used to promote these destinations (Capocchi et al, 2019, 1–6; see also Srnicek, 2017). There is also a suggestion that there is a lack of effective structures of governance in the over-visited destinations, with attempts to limit numbers vehemently opposed by those who are benefiting from expansion. These remarks imply that overtourism is an artificial situation created by an inability or an unwillingness to manage international tourism, and not everyone sees it as a problem, specifically those who profit from it.

Another aspect of overtourism relates to the ineffectiveness of solutions that have been proposed to tackle it. There is a tendency not so much to downplay the problem or deny its existence, but rather to adopt policies that actively extend overtourism instead of limiting its prevalence. This is quite evident in regard to ideas promoted by stakeholder organizations, like the politically influential UNWTO. While it is acknowledged by tourism agencies that certain destinations are receiving too many visitors – to the point where their presence becomes a disruptive influence, eliminating or obscuring the characteristics that made the place attractive in the first place – proposed solutions include measures to distribute visitors across a wider range of sites rather than reduce the tourist population in size (see, for example, UNWTO, 2018). Needless to say, this view is neither helpful nor objective, and potentially encourages even more people to travel, multiplying overtourism rather than curtailing it.

Following on from this point, although the habitually overcrowded cities attract the most headlines, equally important is the diffusion of arrivals to a wider range of destinations, including places that lack the capacity to host large numbers of tourists. This includes the presence of visitors in places not traditionally associated with tourism, especially residential areas, with Airbnb-type letting becoming highly problematic in such neighbourhoods (Cocola Gant and Gago, 2021). Added to this concern is the temporal dispersal of holidaying throughout the calendar year. In the case of Portugal, and no doubt many other countries, this has meant year-round large-scale tourism, stretching far outside the traditional summer season. The impression created is that tourists are everywhere at all times – a more accurate view of overtourism than the ideas promoted by agencies like the UNWTO.

More imaginatively, there is a shift in the meaning of tourism when it is maximized. For visitors, the experience is devalued by overcrowding and other forms of material discomfort; for residents, tourists become a hard-to-manage presence within their communities, posing a threat to local livelihoods and disrupting the character of neighbourhoods. In terms of other aspects of overtourism, the idea that it is commercially important to constantly expand also prevails; this position has been prominent in the Portuguese context, and, superficially, the economic arguments appear very convincing. For instance, according to the most recently published OECD figures, relating to 2018, the tourism sector contributed 8 per cent of gross added value to the Portuguese economy and employed 9 per cent of the working population, taking advantage of the increase in the number of visitors from the Americas and Asia as well as continued popularity among tourists from Brazil, France, Germany, Spain and the UK (OECD, 2020). This quantitative success helps explain why increasing visitor numbers comes to be seen as an intrinsically good thing, regardless of any negative consequences.

In regard to the scale of expansion, statistical evidence on international tourism supports the idea that there was a dramatic rise in foreign visitor numbers during the last decade. Figures from the national statistics agency in Portugal (Figure 3.1) are broadly similar to the UNWTO figures in Figure 1.2, suggesting that the estimated number of arrivals per year peaked at just under 25 million in 2019, then plummeted to just 6.5 million visitors during the first year of the pandemic. Visitor numbers obviously matter a great deal, but another way of looking at the success of expansionism is to consider the amount of revenue being potentially generated by incoming tourists, including their estimated expenditure on hotels and other forms of accommodation during their stays in Portugal.

Figure 3.1: Estimated expenditure of non-resident tourists to Portugal, 2011–20 (Euros, billions)

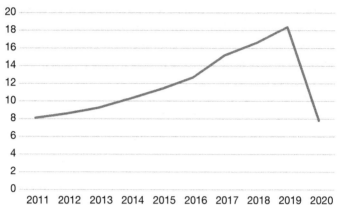

Source: Statistics Portugal (2022) 'Tourism Statistics' [online], Available from: www.ine.pt/xportal/xmain?xpgid=ine_tema&xpid=INE&tema_cod=1713 [accessed 10 February 2022]

Figure 3.1 illustrates the extent of the rise in estimated expenditure levels of tourists coming to Portugal, with a near decade-long period of growth until the abrupt decline in 2020. This graph, along with the breakdowns included in Chapter 1, seems to confirm the success of tourism during this time frame, at least in visitor number and economic terms, and also makes clear the precise point at which expansionism came to an end: the start of the COVID-19 crisis. Given the apparent rapidity of the turnaround, we can see that the pandemic must have come as an extreme shock to the system, although this of course does not mean that the same rate of expansionism would have continued indefinitely.

Overtourism is clearly a complex issue with opponents and supporters. A particular difficulty lies in establishing the optimal level of visitor numbers. Moves to disguise the phenomenon such as spreading tourists to a wider range of sites within the same country and the elongation of tourist seasons are also major concerns, though not necessarily recognized as such.

While there is no agreement about how to tackle the problem, the various sides in this debate can agree on the fact that the pre-pandemic situation was becoming intolerable but the worst-case scenario has now been avoided, ironically, due to the pandemic. Now, the more immediate concern is the sudden downturn in tourism's fortunes and the need to address challenges created by lower visitor numbers.

Undertourism

These reflections take us to the next part of our discussion, which relates to the phenomenon of undertourism. This term, describing problems arising from a lack of visitors, is used much less frequently than 'overtourism'. Research has been limited in scope, and the small number of studies that do exist tend to view undertourism quite literally, and from a tourism industry perspective, as the suboptimal performance of the industry in specific places. Lack of popularity with visitors tends to be explained by what are quite obvious reasons: infrastructure deficits – not having a suitable airport, poorly maintained roads, unserviceable rail links or insufficiently open borders – and past events that have created an image that is off-putting to tourists – including war, terrorism and public health crises (Gowreesunkar and Tan Vo Thanh, 2020, 45–6; see also Seraphin and Gowreesunkar, 2017).

A lack of popularity with visitors is clearly a concern for the industry, but until now undertourism has been seen as a marginal phenomenon, affecting relatively few destinations. We cannot say this about the first two years of the COVID-19 pandemic, as the scale of undertourism was massive due to the huge geographical spread of the virus, affecting practically all forms of international travel for prolonged periods and bringing with it the very real prospect of lasting damage to the tourism industry and other dependent sectors of the economy. Neither can this new form of undertourism be ascribed to limited transportation infrastructure or poor destination image. The outward signs of the new undertourism should by now be familiar to most: the mass cancellation of flights and curtailment of other forms of transportation during the first lockdowns, not to mention the mandatory quarantines, testing procedures, mask wearing and social distancing that continued to make international travel difficult to manage once it had partially restarted.

The inability to continue to expand tourism inevitably raised major concerns for the industry and its existing business model; two years of depressed revenues and lower numbers of incoming visitors. There is also the challenge of restarting full-scale tourism in an industry that divested itself of many skilled employees, who may prove to be hard to replace. This latter issue raises doubts about the wisdom of a rapid return. A risk for countries like Portugal is that there will be a lurch from one extreme to another, with neither undertourism or overtourism being particularly satisfactory positions. It is, then, vital for the tourism industry to find some point of equilibrium in regard to visitor numbers and their temporal and spatial distribution, and we are in fact already seeing signs that this need has been recognized, with the development of tourism oriented around key sustainability concerns.

The tourism industry response

In terms of the methodological approach taken in this book, it is fair to say that like tourists, we have been constrained by circumstances, including the restrictions placed on social interactions. Much of our fieldwork was conducted during the winter of 2021–22, coinciding with the fifth wave of the COVID-19 pandemic in Portugal and the rapid spread of the first of the highly infectious omicron variants. This situation forced us to adapt our methods in order to conduct research using socially distanced and remote methods. For this reason, we need to stress the exploratory nature of our evidence and analysis, having made a deliberate decision to avoid engaging in activities that might be in any way injurious to research subjects. We have, however, been able to build on a wealth of experience in conducting remote fieldwork, gained during earlier stages in the pandemic, which helped us considerably in the development of web-based approaches to study the impact of the crisis (see Cairns et al, 2021a, 2021b; Malet Calvo et al, 2021).

For the remainder of this chapter, we use evidence relating to the management of tourism in Portugal. This was based on engagement with stakeholders in the Portuguese tourism industry alongside exploration of the online discourse generated by various national and regional tourism agencies. Fieldwork involved contacting all the main tourism promotion agencies in Portugal, which cover the offices of national agencies in Lisbon as well as the regions of Alentejo, Algarve, Azores, Central Portugal, Madeira and Porto and the North. We provided online surveys to members of staff about the impact the pandemic has made on their work, with later follow-up questions where clarification was necessary. In regard to time frame, this data was gathered in November and December 2021, with the follow-up questions asked in January 2022.

Coping with the pandemic

We start with an assessment of how agencies coped with the immediate impacts arising from the restrictions placed on international travel from March 2020 onwards. An obvious means of assistance for tourism, especially during the initial months, when there was near total disruption, was the economic support from the state. Looking at the evidence gathered from the ten agencies we surveyed, financial transfers constituted the most immediate means of addressing the problems created by the initial shutdown; for example, to cover the cost of adapting facilities to meet new legal obligations so that when tourists were able to travel, they could be accommodated in a manner that complied with public safety regulations.

In terms of how this support was obtained, industry figures made clear that their requests were grounded in economic expediency and that they needed to remain operational at some level during the shutdowns due to the high importance of tourism to the national economy. This argument is illustrated by the following account from a respondent in one of Portugal's regional agencies:

'Since the beginning of the pandemic, problems were detected in companies with special focus on the tourism sector. ... This was evident right from the start, when in April 2020, the weekly surveys by INE [the national statistics agency] found that 82.2 per cent of companies were in partial or total production, but in tourism, that percentage was 38.3. At the same time, 31.7 per cent of all companies reported a drop in turnover of more than 75 per cent, while in tourism the percentage was 71.1. And 29.5 per cent of companies indicated a reduction in staff in service of more than 75 per cent, while in tourism it was 64.6 per cent.'

The message being sent to us as researchers was that the tourism industry endured a disproportionate level of 'suffering' arising from the public health restrictions imposed on international travel, and this position is in line with the figures from Portugal's national statistics agency cited earlier in this chapter (see Figure 3.1). Figures also show that other sectors of the economy were comparatively unaffected by the restrictions at this time and presumably did not need the same levels of support, implying that more assistance could have been given to tourism. This point is developed by a respondent from one of Portugal's largest regional tourism agencies:

'There are challenges in tourism that are not present in other industries, since we work directly with people who are travelling to Portugal from all over the world.

This is not like the construction industry, which was allowed to continue during the periods of lockdown, or manufacturing, where some minor adjustments could be made to keep people in factories safe.'

Another respondent, from a national agency based in Lisbon, emphasized the important interconnections tourism has with other sectors of the economy. This means that the impact of government support to tourism can multiply its importance by helping to hold together crucial parts of the larger economic infrastructure: "Tourism is a vitally important industry to the Portuguese economy. There are also the industries that depend on tourism, especially hospitality and all the supply chains. So, when you help the tourist industry, you are helping these sectors as well."

Taken at face value, this positioning is highly effective. A multilayered argument is established, maximizing the importance of the tourism industry to the national economy, both in financial terms and through its status as an employer and part of a greater chain of financial dependency. We can also see how the tourism industry uses statistics pragmatically, including the Portuguese government's own figures, which the state will presumably not contest. If we were being more cynical, it could be pointed out that in estimating the extent of losses due to the pandemic, comparisons are being made to the peak levels of tourism that preceded the emergency – the over-tourism situation that brought its own set of problems for local communities. Looking further back in time, we might even argue that what happened in 2020 was merely a return to the levels of tourism before the expansionist decade. As such, the downturn could credibly be interpreted as a reversion to the mean rather than an 'unnatural' contraction. Regardless of how we perceive the situation, the amount of financial support provided by the state was never going to be equivalent to the losses from the absence of international visitors, although tourism agency staff were generally satisfied to know that their special position within the economy had been recognized by the state.

In terms of other forms of support, we have various accounts of exactly what was provided during the first year of the pandemic in addition to money to maintain the integrity of the industry. For example, a respondent from another regional tourism agency explained to us what had been made available to her organization: "Given this [pandemic] panorama, several instruments and support measures were made available, that can be summarized around three essential objectives: cash flow support, investment support and support to maintain jobs. These instruments can also be divided between transversal support to the economy and specific support for the tourism sector."

In explaining what this arrangement entailed, some forms of support were provided to a wide range of sectors of the economy in Portugal, including lay-off schemes to pay employees for not working. Specifically for tourism, non-refundable transfers were distributed via the aptly named Adapt Programme, which at first made money available for the purchase of personal protective equipment (masks, acrylics, dispensers, and so on) and then, as mentioned previously, provided a fund for the adaptation of tourist activities to comply with the new health and safety guidelines. Such was the popularity of this programme, the original budget allocation of 5 million euros was exhausted within 24 hours and later had to be increased to 10 million euros. Interest-free loans were also made available to small and medium-sized businesses in the tourism sector, with a one-year grace period. The repayment process was overseen by Turismo de Portugal, and the time limit was later extended due to the persisting problems in the economy.

Taking these accounts at face value, the investment made by the state in tourism at this time appears quite reasonable and, if we accept the industry's view of its importance to the economy in Portugal, logical. From the tourism industry's own point of view, their lobbying was not cynical, but rather an example of people in a hard-pressed situation doing their job effectively, with a view to retaining jobs in very difficult circumstances; it is not their duty to be the arbiters of some kind of objective truth about the actual economic value of tourism. From the state's perspective, in making what are in reality fairly token gestures – providing millions of euros where billions appear to have been lost (see also Nhamo et al, 2020) – the Portuguese government was seen to be doing something about the pandemic and its impact on the national economy, when in fact it was doing relatively little beyond supporting a few placeholding measures, such as the creation of digital platforms to convey the message that the interruption to international travel is temporary.

The sustainability response

Moving on from questions of financial support, we might want to consider other, less prominent developments that have taken place in the tourism industry during the pandemic, particularly as the crisis moved into its second year. In the case of Portugal, this included addressing sustainability issues, acknowledging the negative impact made by international travel on the environment. While growing in prominence in this national context, this strategy is aligned with contemporaneous developments at international level, reflected in discourse on platforms hosted by the UNWTO, which has helped to make sustainability a 'core tenet' of the industry (Yang et al, 2021, 8). At the national level, Turismo de Portugal published the '+Sustainable Tourism 20–23' plan, centred on making tourist resorts energy-efficient in terms of water and waste management systems; the agency is also looking at ways of reducing the use of single-use plastics by international visitors.

Looking at the evidence we have been able to gather, the impression created is that the main focus of the tourism industry in Portugal has been on attaining a more equal geographical distribution of foreign tourists, suggesting alignment with the view of overtourism promoted by the UNWTO discussed previously rather than any attempt to engage in the 'degrowth' processes that have been suggested by some commentators as an alternate solution (see, for example, Fletcher et al, 2019; Higgins-Desbiolles et al, 2019). The position among tourism industry agencies in Portugal can be summed up as wanting to maintain, or even increase, visitor numbers at national level via their regional diffusion; the extra numbers are to be directed towards the less visited inland destinations, which appear to have been suffering from the old form of undertourism, thus helping them reach some kind of parity with the popular beach resorts and coastal cities. Needless to say, this approach was endorsed by tourism agencies based in the less visited regions:

> 'As I mentioned, this agency aims for a better temporal and spatial distribution of tourism demand, opting in all circumstances to acquire local services in all the supply chains of the local or regional tourism sector. This involves promoting, valuing and incorporating in its offer seasonal and endogenous products of a diverse nature – from food products to burel derivatives. We are consistently promoting regional brands that by their nature promote and incorporate sustainable elements ... incorporating, whenever possible, the promotion or use of sustainable mobility.'

As found in UNWTO discourse, we can also observe the deployment of the idea of making tourism a year-round activity in a wider range of places, alongside emphasis on the industry's value to regional economies. In the case of the respondent just quoted, this related to the sale of burel, a traditional Portuguese textile made from pure sheep wool, manufactured in the region of Serra da Estrela (the highest mountain range in Portugal), traditionally associated with shepherds. We might, then, argue that this is a form of sustainability grounded in economic imperatives as well as, or rather than, pure environmentalism.

Assessing this position, and taking into account the challenges that have arisen for the tourism industry during the pandemic, we might also see regional diversification as part of the process of adapting to changing demands from consumers. The approach provides an opportunity to take advantage of the presence of fewer international tourists. This shift in emphasis is present not only in our evidence but also in materials published on digital platforms as part of pandemic-era promotional campaigns, extending to efforts made to contain the virus being presented as part of the appeal of rural Portugal.

During the pandemic, Turismo de Portugal published information online to help keep prospective customers informed about the unfolding situation within the industry, including the current state of restrictions and the sanitary measures put in place, to provide reassurance to reluctant travellers. The idea, then, was that by making the 'problem' visible it could be seen to have been managed, with potential visitors able to make informed decisions about travelling, adjusting their expectations in the process. This proposition was also present in online marketing materials published on the VisitPortugal platform (www.visitportugal.com). The message being transmitted informed potential customers, literally, that 'You are safe with us. Breathe deeply and enjoy'. VisitPortugal was thus able to make very good use of the relative peace and quiet inadvertently created by the relative emptiness of the pandemic, which is now marketed as an integral part of the country's appeal.

The message has been further integrated into online initiatives at national and regional levels in Portugal. This includes portals mentioned by the agency respondents, Better Dreams Ahead (www.bdacenterofportugal.com) and Embrace You Soon (embraceyousoon.com), directed at international and local markets. In regard to content, alongside depictions of holiday possibilities, these platforms reflect concerns that have featured prominently in news agendas, including environmental activism. For example, on Better Dreams Ahead, we can read the story of how the tourism industry has declared a climate emergency, implying an alignment between tourism and environmentalism. Meanwhile, Embrace You Soon, a site hosted by the Central Portugal tourism agency, takes a gentler approach, emphasizing the bucolic joys of the country's inland destinations. The agency's very attractive message – alongside pictures of clear blue skies and luscious vegetation – provides a contrast to the chaos of urban life, that has been further complicated in cities by the demands of a seemingly endless public health crisis. Lest anyone miss this subtext, the message is made clear in accompanying text: 'Ironically, quarantine has given us that most precious commodity: time. For us and for ourselves. It's time to take a deep breath and discover life. Once we start travelling again, we will do it slowly. To enjoy life to the full. Without rushing.'

We can, then, see some signs of a convergence between long-standing sustainability concerns and the need to address undertourism, both in its traditional form and the new variety associated with the pandemic. The main focus is now on the enrichment of the international travel experience, inadvertently made more exclusive by the decline in visitor numbers at national level, and potential environmental gains through less intensive use of aviation and other forms of polluting transportation.

Summary

The preceding discussion takes us towards some final reflections on overtourism and undertourism, and the integration of the issue of sustainability into the marketing of tourism in Portugal during the pandemic. Most obviously, we can appreciate that the pandemic constitutes an end to the expansionism of the recent past, even if the stoppage is neither absolute nor permanent. Fewer people have been travelling, and two years on from the start of the crisis, tourist numbers remain short of pre-pandemic peak levels, with long-haul travel remaining particularly problematic for the industry. New problems are also emerging, including the threat posed by the war in Ukraine and genuine concerns about the capacity of airports in formerly popular destinations to cope with a sudden return to pre-pandemic visitor levels.

In Portugal, there remains within the tourism industry, and no doubt in other mobility-dependent sectors of the economy, the need to find an equilibrium between overtourism and undertourism, avoiding having too many or not enough visitors, and a solution of sorts has been found in the idea of sustainability, with the industry encouraging people to visit places with fewer tourists, although this is still in its tentative stages. This approach can also involve making use of Portugal's natural resources, with tranquil stays in inland destinations particularly appealing, making rural tourism an important area for future investigation.

FOUR

International Student Mobility and Immobility

This chapter looks at another form of international travel greatly affected by the COVID-19 pandemic: the mobility of tertiary education students. Again, the focus is on the Portuguese context, and as in Chapter 3, the discussion engages with developments before and after the start of the crisis, with the decade prior to the pandemic characterized by a sustained period of expansion, followed by uncertainty. However, as suggested by the statistics presented in Chapter 1, while the status of short-term exchanges – credit mobility – is unclear due to limitations in the data, there are some signs that levels of student migration to Portugal actually increased during the pandemic.

Such developments reflect the fact that the country has a distinct international student mobility profile, perhaps different to the European norm, having become a destination for visitors from neighbouring nations, via programmes such as the European Commission-supported Erasmus platform, as well as those from farther afield, including Africa, Asia and the Americas, with many of these students staying in Portugal for long durations (Sin et al, 2017; França and Cairns, 2020; Malet Calvo et al, 2020). As noted in prior research on this topic, it may have been logical for these latter students to stay in place after the start of the crisis due to a lack of opportunities to return to societies more deeply affected by the pandemic (Cairns et al, 2021a; 2021b; Malet Calvo et al, 2021).

Looking at the broader picture, we also wish to contribute to the student mobility research field. The topic generated a huge volume of academic studies and grey literature during the 'mobility turn' era (see Chapter 2). This material suggests that there has been an expansion and a diversification of the internationalized learning experience, which came to integrate formal, informal and non-formal pedagogies as a means of generating valuable forms of mobility capital (Cairns 2021a, 2021b). For this reason, having already looked at some of the available statistics in Chapter 1, the main part of this chapter focuses on the qualitative impact of the COVID-19 pandemic, reflecting on international student life at the most intensive periods of lockdown. With the benefit of two years' hindsight, we can now see that a devaluation of the internationalized learning experience took place during the first wave of the pandemic, with less mobility capital generated by students and higher costs for host universities due to the increased duty of care. Also noted in this part of the discussion is the main means by which student mobility, and academic life in general, continued during the pandemic: the use of digital platforms for the delivery of teaching and support services. This resulted in a rediscovery of the idea of virtual mobility.

Expansionism in student mobility

Like tourism, student mobility expanded considerably in scale and scope in the years preceding the pandemic. Before this time, spending time at a foreign university was something of a rarity, to the point of being seen as an elitist practice, with social distinction generated from the exceptionality of the experience (Murphy-Lejeune, 2002). The value of mobility started to change as many more students began to travel, with fixed-duration exchange visits becoming if not the norm, then far from exceptional, especially in the EU, where the focus was on generating intercultural skills via relatively short stays abroad. At the same time as this form of expansionism was taking place, students continued to move abroad for longer durations, attracted by the prospect of gaining credentials at universities with globally recognized reputations. These two developments coalesced into a twofold model of international student mobility, centred on what came to be described by various authors as 'credit mobility' and 'diploma mobility' or 'degree mobility' (see, for example, Brooks and Waters, 2011).

Since this time, this dual model has been superseded, and it is recognized that many other pathways are now open to people seeking international student mobility, referred to as 'learning mobility' in European policy discourse, a term that encompasses not only undergraduates and postgraduates but also trainees, volunteers and individuals on work placements, vocational programmes or staff exchanges, to name but a few of the most prominent examples. This diversification was consolidated by the rebranding in 2014 of the European Commission-supported Erasmus programme, somewhat literally, as Erasmus+. Hence, as was the case with tourism (see Chapter 3), student mobility became multifaceted and widely diffused, although the main focus in the EU still appeared to be on relatively short fixed-duration stays. These developments raised levels of incoming and outgoing movement in many European countries and increased the number of institutions hosting educational visitors.

This critical mass of mobility also attained geopolitical importance. In addition to programmes like Erasmus being seen as a kind of exercise in EU soft power, capable of spreading European values throughout its member states and beyond, the internationalized learning experience was looked on by the European Commission as an opportunity to subtly intervene in young people's careers, focusing on heightening their international employability and strengthening interculturality through the geodemographically diverse conviviality that 'naturally' happens during stays abroad (Cairns et al, 2017). For higher education institutions, involvement in student mobility may have been more pragmatic; it was a means of gathering funds from fee-paying overseas students, with other forms of mobility used to enhance universities' internationalization profiles within what had become a highly competitive marketplace, reflecting a neoliberal philosophy that is ubiquitous in tertiary education (see also Bok, 2009). As with tourism, marketing strategies gained prominence, with universities branding themselves as chic destinations for fee-paying student migrants. This led to an obsession with strategic planning, performance indicators and corporate image (Komljenovic and Robertson, 2016). Finally, like the tourism industry, universities stressed the importance of attracting foreign students to boost national economies, viewing themselves as generators of wealth from tuition fees and subsidiary activities such as the provision of student accommodation (Malet Calvo et al, 2020, 130–1).

All these developments help explain the appeal of expanded student mobilities, but this does not of course mean that every aspect of the system functioned perfectly. In fact, major disparities emerged out of the international contest between universities to attract visitors and send as many of their own students as possible abroad; some institutions succeeded in mobilizing their students, while others struggled to find sufficient numbers who wanted to travel, leading them to accept subsidiary positions as dormitory destinations. A lack of balance in levels of incoming and outgoing mobility, partly a reflection of international disparities in levels of support on offer to students, brought about a core–periphery dynamic within Europe that risked creating new forms of social exclusion in programmes like Erasmus, which were, ironically, marketed in terms of their ability to deliver social inclusion (Cairns, 2017). This explains why the expansionism that characterized the pre-pandemic period can only be considered a partial success. As was the case with tourism, problems tended to arise in places that became too popular with visitors, especially where there was limited capacity in local housing markets, suggesting a variant on the overtourism phenomenon discussed in the previous chapter.

Mobility capital and fractional migrants

As suggested in the preceding paragraphs, student mobility in the EU was extended to a wide range of learning contexts, not just traditional academic courses. In practice, this involved a fusion of formal, informal and non-formal learning in the programmes of Erasmus+ and other smaller-scale platforms. The popularity of the approach suggests quantitative success, with (as noted in Chapter 1) an estimated 640,000 people studying, training or volunteering abroad in 2020, according to Erasmus+ publicity materials.[1]

While we can write about this issue in terms of numbers participating, we also need to consider the implications for education and training systems arising from the blending of different learning formats, and the prospects for generating and strengthening certain aspects of mobility capital, including interculturality and international employability. As we have detailed in previous publications, this is quite a convoluted process, the idea being to produce mobility capital out of a reflexive learning process and build competencies and skills that establish a capacity to work productively with people from a range of different backgrounds (see Cairns, 2021a, 2021b). While hard to achieve – and not easy to explain – these forms of mobility capital are outcomes from a synergy implicit in the internationalized learning experience, differentiating it from forms of travel that are explicitly oriented around more immediate forms of gratification; that is to say, the prospect of gaining mobility capital is what distinguishes learning mobility from travelling for a holiday. A distinction is also drawn between the classical idea of a migrant moving abroad with a view to increasing their economic capital and the mobile subject who can defer capitalizing on the experience until an unspecified later time.

Recognizing that a pursuit of mobility capital is taking place helps explain why mobility opportunities are being provided for a wide range of audiences, including young people participating in civil society or sports-related projects. While this diffusion of mobility to non-academic contexts is not problematic in itself, and may be beneficial for many participants, it is valid to ask just how much mobility capital can be generated in stays abroad that last for only a few days or weeks, as is common in mobility projects in the youth field (see also Allaste and Nugin, 2021). On the other hand, these short visits might function as an entrée to more substantial visits that would not have been contemplated otherwise. We might, then, regard a lot of the non-academic mobility that takes place in programmes like Erasmus+ as a form of preliminary learning rather than mobility in its own right.

More concerning is the impact of these fragmented mobilities on ontological development, and the threat posed to incipient transitions to the labour market, which can be needlessly interrupted or elongated by multiple stays abroad. This issue is discussed elsewhere in relation to involvement in international internships: Cuzzocrea and Cairns (2020) found that while many interns enjoyed the experience of living in some of Europe's most cosmopolitan cities, they also tended to find themselves stuck in a kind of exclusion loop, since the promised entry to an international career eluded them due to their position as eternal outsiders. This led people to accept one internship after another in the hope that the next trip would be the one to take them to a point of job security, an expensive tactic in cities like Brussels, London and Paris. The volume of accumulated time spent abroad can also create a feeling of rootlessness and detachment – a separation not only from the places they had left but also in the host community, into which they never quite fit. This explains why, despite appearing to exercise an agency of sorts in regard to mobility choices, these fractional migrants experience problems that can affect their sense of self and physical well-being, especially when it becomes difficult to access health care and other forms of welfare.

Precarious learning

A further aspect of the internationalization process concerns the learning experience itself. As previously intimated, a relatively novel aspect of programmes like Erasmus is the use of pedagogies that capitalize on the international conviviality 'naturally' generated within a group of co-resident students from different national and regional backgrounds, facilitated by the blending of formal education with extracurricular activities. The idea is that people learn how to be mobile from the other mobile people they encounter during their stays abroad, who then pass their wisdom on to the next arrivals. Significantly, much of this learning takes place outside the classroom, in a range of social settings and in the domestic sphere.

Researchers view such arrangements as leading to the creation of a kind of 'bubble'; a space in which the main points of reference for intercultural learning are fellow travellers, not local people or professional educators (Cuzzocrea et al, 2021; see also Earls, 2018). Such bubbles facilitate generation of the aforementioned forms of mobility capital, but with limitations. If an international student's social universe is limited to peers participating in the same or similar programmes, and perhaps those studying at the same university or living in the same accommodation, the form of cosmopolitanism produced will be quite artificial. This brings to mind a critique of student mobility expressed in existentialist terms, with their place in a host society seen as alienating 'stranger' (Murphy-Lejeune, 2002). The historical critique in Murphy-Lejeune's book is rather harsh when applied to the present, since it assumes a homogeneity of the study abroad experience that is no longer the case due to expansionism and diversification. Furthermore, students can find themselves distanced from peers and host country networks due to their lack of social and economic resources, a situation related to the high costs of learning mobility and/or the fact that they are making financial sacrifices in order to pursue their 'mobility dreams' (Cairns et al, 2017, 3).

It is, then, important to remember that relatively undocumented problems emerged within the international student population during the time of expansionism, and that within this population, we have people with different levels of affluence, and inevitably, some international students will be in vulnerable positions due to their limited resources. Thus, we might characterize expanded mobility as incorporating an element of precarious learning, and precarious learners.

International student immobility

These remarks about vulnerability and precarity take us towards the turning point of the pandemic, and the impact of immobility on mobile students, a point in time when the learning bubble appears to have burst. In the case of tertiary education, this included a transformation of the materiality of learning and a change in the spaces in which international students live and learn. Traditionally, they experience a form of blended learning, combining formal, informal and non-formal pedagogies, and all three components contribute towards making the exercise a success. Studying abroad is not simply a case of obtaining credit for academic work, but also a geographical widening of a participant's social network and possibly a broadening and opening up of the mind.

This may also entail moving outside the learning bubble and into the host community and the host university due to the volume and density of information that needs to be conveyed to establish intercultural connections and avoid the kind of alienation experiences detailed in historical studies of student mobility. During the lockdown stages of the pandemic, as well as the informal and non-formal aspects of this learning process being curtailed, formal education was transplanted into the spaces formerly occupied by the other pedagogies. This constitutes a huge change in what might be described as the materiality of internationalized higher education, one that was perhaps impossible to manage (see also Brooks and Waters, 2018). What happens, then, when internationalized learning becomes a highly insular experience? Expansionism in international student mobility also meant that when the pandemic began, more people were affected than would have been the case in previous times, creating difficulties for host institutions and funding agencies as well as students.[2]

While a potential decline in numbers of exchange students is a serious concern, just as important is the impact on pedagogies reliant on a high degree of international conviviality. Added to this is the social impact for students, arising from the restrictions that became an integral part of pandemic life for many months. This impact has obviously been transversal, not specific to international students; but those in precarious positions may have endured additional stress, lacking a firm grounding in the host country's support networks. This explains why economic challenges emerged for such students at this time, a topic featuring prominently in prior work with members of this cohort in Portugal (see especially the accounts discussed in Cairns et al, 2021b).

Universities also faced awkward questions in regard to how (much) student mobility should be allowed or encouraged at times when travel is problematized, taking into account both public safety concerns and the need to preserve the economic integrity of learning programmes; continuing to invite large numbers of students risked spreading the virus, but restricting numbers would potentially undo the progress made in expanding participation prior to the pandemic. An additional concern we might also want to acknowledge relates to the ramifications of expanded use of digital platforms for the delivery of teaching and support services, extending to a rediscovery of the idea of virtual mobility, providing us with an opportunity to assess some of the strengths and weaknesses of remote learning formats.

The first wave of immobility

Before considering the possible longer-term consequences arising from immobility in internationalized tertiary education, especially for host institutions, it is worth looking back at the initial months of the crisis and revisiting evidence from the Portuguese research context to illustrate some of the difficulties and controversies that emerged during the most stringent periods of lockdown. Since this evidence has already been discussed in a number of journal articles (see Cairns et al, 2021b; Malet Calvo et al, 2021), we limit ourselves to highlighting a few of the most prominent findings, at times rethinking earlier conclusions with the benefit of almost two years of hindsight.[3]

The initial months of the COVID-19 pandemic were characterized by the rapid shutdown of societies, including the closure of university facilities and the cancellation of international and interregional travel, and at times extending to limited movement within neighbourhoods. In universities, the measures adopted to cope with the situation differed, but generally involved restricting access to campuses and moving learning online, with the results of this shift detailed in the findings of a range of studies from across the world (see, for example, Pham and Ho, 2020; Agasisti and Soncin, 2021; de Boer, 2021; Mok et al, 2021; Veerasamy and Ammigan, 2021; Yang and Huang, 2021; Moscaritolo et al, 2022). The impression created by this large body of scholarship is that the international student world shrank, with major concerns for universities arising from the sudden contraction of catchment areas and the potential decline in recruitment. Researchers of human mobility were also interested in finding out more about students' experiences at this time given that, almost overnight, their 'super-mobile' (Czerska-Shaw and Krzaklewska, 2021a) worlds were turned inside out. However, while there was considerable confusion, now-immobilized students tended to adapt quickly to the changing situation, albeit recognizing that they were not able to enjoy an experience that corresponded to their pre-pandemic expectations.

This position is echoed in findings emerging from our own research experience. Through the use of online methods to gather evidence at this time, it was possible to conduct 27 interviews with international students in Portugal between April and June 2020, the first lockdown, including credit mobility students and longer-term student migrants from Africa, Europe and South America. Reflecting on the main outcomes, two specific insights were hard to ignore. A first observation relates to international students' experiences of living through the most intensive periods of lockdown, which involved a dramatic change in lifestyle and learning routine due to university closures and social restrictions as well as limited travel possibilities. These conditions created a kind of externally enforced insularity, to the point of posing an ontological threat to students whose lives were previously defined by the freedom to move, often in a relatively spontaneous manner. A second observation relates to the negative impact on mental and physical health. This form of stress is obviously different to that experienced when coping with financial difficulties – although economic and emotional matters can be linked – and one that crosses socio-demographic lines. In other words, it was not just people in economically vulnerable positions who suffered, but a much broader range of individuals, for whom the pandemic came as a profound culture shock that no one had adequately prepared for (see also Elmer et al, 2020).

In summarizing this position, we might say that international student life came to be characterized by rising economic and emotional costs. It takes a great deal of money to sustain a stay abroad, and the sudden onset of immobility brought a new range of conspicuous costs – for instance, where educational courses were prolonged or needed to be repeated (see also Carolan et al, 2020). Among less well-off students, there were the additional stresses of coping with lost income, as many part-time jobs ceased to exist with the pandemic; some felt compelled to absorb these losses by finding new jobs, working in local supermarkets, courier services or hospitals instead of the now-shuttered restaurants and bars, all of which brought significantly more risk of exposure to the virus. We might also add that some of the defining features of learning abroad – especially the ability to engage with people from different backgrounds and to explore new places, especially the host city (Zazina and Nowakowska, 2022) – were severely affected, creating a very hollow experience indeed.

Immobilized higher education

How, then, are we to make sense of what happened in internationalized higher education at this time? In Chapter 2, it was implied that the expansion of various mobilities – including the international circulation of students – could be seen as part of a broader mobility turn, with authors such as John Urry recognizing the significance of mobilities in transforming social and economic life. The success of this approach seems to have been predicated on relatively free circulation of people, meaning that during a period of immobilization, problems would emerge.

The evidence summarized in the previous section confirms the existence of practical difficulties created by the sudden onset of immobility in the Portuguese context, as well as the harder-to-quantify feelings of anxiety and isolation among students whose lives were previously defined by a strong cosmopolitan disposition. This is not just a question of consuming less mobility or experiencing more complicated travel processes, but also a possible shift in the meaning of learning mobility, making what was once anticipated as a relatively pleasurable experience into a hardship to be endured. These were the impressions at the time during which these changes were taking place. With the benefit of hindsight, we can now see that this shift was neither absolute nor irreversible, and as early as the second year of the pandemic, student mobility regained significant ground, while student migration numbers were less affected in our national context, and even increased (see Figure 1.3). This form of migration was not alone in withstanding the pandemic. As we discuss in Chapter 5, labour migration continued throughout this time, albeit not without its own difficulties. We can then deduce that a certain amount of stoicism is present among students and others moving abroad for prolonged periods, who generally stayed in place when the pandemic hit; they did so for many reasons, including the difficulty of abandoning a degree course in progress and the limited or non-existent prospect of returning home.

The impact of the pandemic on short-duration mobilities appears to have been more elastic. There were obviously fewer people participating in Erasmus–type exchanges during the first wave of infections, and some who had travelled before the initial outbreak were able to return home before the anticipated end of their visit, one reason being the relative ease with which students from neighbouring countries could travel. While we do not have comprehensive statistics at the time of writing, reports within our own university suggest a drop in incoming Erasmus students of at least 50 per cent in 2020–21. There does seem, however, to have been a concerted effort to maintain the integrity of internationalized learning programmes, with universities continuing to host meaningful levels of students even during the first year of the crisis, a time during which domestic students generally worked at home. This might, on the surface, be seen as a positive development, although it would be interesting to learn what people who engaged in Erasmus at a time of restricted internal and external mobility actually gained from the experience.

Virtual mobility

With the benefit of hindsight, much of what was stated in our previous articles was obvious in respect to the changes that took place in international student life during the early months of the pandemic, and this really does not need to be repeated beyond a few reminders. Confinement in cramped accommodation. Anxieties about friends and family back home. Doubts about continuing with studies and the occasional rushed return home. Another common experience which does, however, merit some additional comment concerns the large-scale move to learning online, with lectures and other forms of teaching being conducted via the internet. This form of remote learning is not a new phenomenon in tertiary education, with many countries having 'open university'-type institutions or other forms of long-distance learning. However, prior to the pandemic, the use of online platforms in internationalized higher education was limited. In regard to learning mobility programmes, virtual activities were in fact confined to specific, and relatively peripheral, aspects of the experience, such as orientation prior to departure and follow-up procedures after returning home. The pandemic obviously resulted in a rethink of this approach, with virtual mobility now acting as a placeholder for students who were unable or reluctant to travel but still wanted to obtain some kind of internationalization accreditation, with remote learning also used by those who had already moved abroad before the first wave and others who came after the crisis had started. However, if reports within our university are to be believed, the entire virtual mobility experience seems to have been only briefly considered as a viable alternative.

Its unpopularity can be explained by a lack of enthusiasm, and exhaustion, among teachers and the impracticality of delivering pastoral support to students through online platforms. Also evident from our prior research was the poor quality of facilities many overseas students had at 'home', with limited access to laptops and low-quality internet connections, not to mention overcrowding in shared accommodation, making participation in online classes an additional challenge. At a more practical level, online pedagogies provide limited scope for encouraging the kinds of interculturality and internationalized employability discussed previously due to the lack of opportunities for engaging in international conviviality. It was, therefore, no surprise that in the later waves of the pandemic, students in universities largely stayed on campus rather than working in their temporary homes, despite the risks they posed to each other and to academic staff.

Return to mobile learning

Those reflections take us to the final part of this chapter – empirically informed perspectives about how mobility has been managed at universities during the pandemic. Having tempered the somewhat downbeat assessment of immobility in higher education that characterized our work in the initial months of the crisis (Cairns et al, 2021c) with the realization that, on the surface, not as much has changed as we might have anticipated, it perhaps time for a rethink. Despite the highly visible problems, substantial numbers of students continued to travel, even during the most intensive periods of lockdown. So when talking about a return to mobility, the quantitative changes might not have been as profound as they could have been after the initial drop-off in circulation levels. However, this impression disguises the deeper impacts, what might be described as the qualitative impacts of the pandemic, including continuing problems with international travel and questions about the quality of the learning experience.

This is not an easy issue to assess. Host universities are reluctant to concede that they have problems, concerned about damaging their hard-won internationalization profiles by deterring visitors, and losing much-needed revenue. To explore this issue, we have looked at how universities in Portugal restarted mobility during the pandemic, or enabled its continuance, drawing on evidence collected from 20 universities across the country. As fieldwork was conducted at a time of renewed restrictions on social contacts, during the fifth wave of the pandemic in the late months of 2021, as was the case with the empirical work discussed in Chapter 3, all research had to be conducted remotely. Data collection involved the distribution of a questionnaire to university staff members located in international departments or units dedicated to the Erasmus programme, with later follow-up questions delivered via the internet. Given the limited scope of this evidence, we give only a brief assessment here, but we try to look beyond the more self-evident issues – such as the initial drop in numbers of credit mobility exchanges in the first year of the pandemic and the relative stability of overseas enrolments – and focus on less prominent findings in relation to the future place of remote learning.

Pastoral care

While the respondents had relatively little to say about the impact of the pandemic on the academic performance of students, perhaps a reflection of their primary role as university administrators, a major concern related to the delivery of support services. This process became complicated at the start of the pandemic as a result of the need to respect public health guidelines as well as the understandable reticence of students and staff to take part in in-person activities. Most straightforward was the provision of information via the internet, both to visiting students in situ and those in other countries who had travelled to universities outside Portugal before the lockdown started. This seems to have been accomplished without too many difficulties. One form of support was the offer of online assistance to those studying abroad who wished to return home, as explained by one respondent in a university in the north of Portugal:

'We tried to keep the outward students informed about the situation at home. As Portugal was not severely affected during the early months of the pandemic, it made sense for students in countries where there were greater numbers of infections to return. So, we tried to answer any questions they had about how they could do this without losing credit for the work they had already completed.'

We can see that this was a relatively straightforward case of deciding which country – the host destination or the sending society – offered the best prospects for coping with the pandemic at this time. In some ways, this was a balancing exercise in regard to the severity of the public health emergency, also recognizing the need to avoid punishing students for failing to complete their studies and losing course accreditation for pandemic-related reasons. However, in respect to outgoing mobility from Portugal, the impression created by our evidence is that returns from abroad were the exception, with most students staying in the host country until they had completed their studies as planned, by which time more travel options were available.

The need to provide information seems to have abated in the later stage of the pandemic. Understandably, at the beginning, students wanted to be kept up to date about conditions at home and abroad, including travel options and the status of their educational courses where there were interruptions to study plans. However, students soon became adept at keeping themselves informed about what was happening particularly after the more stringent social restrictions were lifted and people could socialize once more, making life much easier for the host universities. The impression created among the staff members we engaged with is that there was also a relatively rapid adaptation to the changing circumstances among international students (see also Czerska-Shaw and Krzaklewska, 2021b), meaning that it was only during the first two or three months of the crisis that major difficulties were encountered.

Virtual solutions

Another issue for university staff during times of lockdown was the awkwardness of using virtual platforms as a means of supplementing or substituting in-person teaching, with some teachers doing this for the first time. This move was very unpopular, with online learning seen as a poor substitute for the 'real thing', but accepted out of necessity. Staff members also acknowledged the limitations of online formats for teaching and, more specifically, the lack of opportunities for developing certain aspects of intercultural competency. As one respondent from a university in central Portugal explained: "Mobility is physical and must be experience[d] in all its richness only in this way, which goes far beyond scientific learning. European citizenship can only be achieved in this way. Virtual mobility is an extra, excellent for short mobilities, but it does not replace the physical mobility at all."

However, within some other universities we engaged with, there was a greater degree of pragmatism and a somewhat different attitude on display. Having developed virtual teaching platforms during lockdowns, it was implied that such approaches would continue to be used by some international students. However, this was seen not as a replacement but, rather, a supplement to in-person mobility, and a means of enrolling students who were not willing or able to travel due to their personal circumstances. As one interviewee said:

> 'No, with the virtual mobility, it is a different experience. Students will always want to travel and to experience the different aspects of life in another country. Not just teaching but the food and the different culture. It is not possible to do these things online. But we recognize that the online approach is better for some people. For example, where they do not have the money to travel or if they have family responsibilities at home.'

In this sense, virtual mobility might be seen as a means to reignite expansionism through creating a new and quite separate stratum of internationalized higher education. While there may be some benefits in relation to social inclusivity, what underpins this development, in addition to possibly wanting to include people for whom international travel is impractical, is the wish to recruit more fee-paying students. We might, then, see virtual mobility as a means not only to include more people but also to generate greater revenues, and in a manner that is potentially safe and less injurious to the environment than existing approaches, echoing the sustainability theme mentioned in Chapter 4.

One other important finding emerging from our research is that virtual mobility was already envisaged as becoming a reality before the pandemic, possibly forming part of the next phase of the Erasmus+ programme. The programme was prolonged for the years 2021–27, but this was in the planning stages long before the first lockdowns began. This suggests that there has already been a substantial degree of alignment between, on the one hand, what universities want, and on the other, the wishes of funding agencies like the European Commission. We might credit them with a certain amount of prescience, since no one predicted that a pandemic would come along and momentarily increase the demand for online teaching. This is obviously an issue that we need to monitor carefully in future studies on this topic, but we can already see that virtual mobility may grow in importance even as we move out of the pandemic, becoming the next important revenue stream for universities.

Maintaining future mobility

Given that the situation we are exploring is still in flux, we cannot realistically draw definitive conclusions about the future of student mobility, virtual or otherwise. We can, however, see that while there has been major disruption to learning mobility, universities in Portugal seem to have managed the initial trauma reasonably well, adapting to what were unpredictable circumstances, as have their international students. This is confirmed by the available statistics, with credit mobility exchanges affected in the initial stages of the emergency – unsurprisingly considering the lack of opportunities for international travel – but rebounding relatively rapidly (see Figure 1.5). Longer-duration degree enrolments seem to have been relatively unaffected, with numbers of incoming students actually increasing according to the statistics presented in Chapter 1. This suggests that, despite the difficulties created by the pandemic, there was no serious change in regard to student migration numbers at this time.

Notwithstanding this apparent optimism, we should use the experience of the recent moratorium to examine some of the more problematic aspects of student mobility, including issues arising from existing and emerging fault lines. During the expansionist period, student mobility could re-enforce inequalities along both social and geographical vectors, with some countries, and certain universities, becoming adept at maximizing numbers of outgoing students, while other places emerged as attractive destinations for incoming learners, with Portugal in the latter position. It remains to be seen how this arrangement will hold up, especially at a time when the cost of student mobility is going to increase considerably due to the rising cost of living in both sending and receiving countries. Funding agencies, like the European Commission and the many private and public foundations that operate student exchange platforms need to become much more generous in their financial support, even if this means fewer people travelling. Student migrants meanwhile need recognition of their status as citizens and full access to health and other forms of welfare, a debate we explore in a somewhat different context in the next chapter.

Summary

To recap, the impact of the immobility turn in higher education appears to have been time-limited, partial and perhaps reversible – that is, if we accept the version of events indicated by the available statistics, including those presented in Chapter 1. That there are discrepancies between different data sources – European Commission statistics present a different narrative to that put forward by enrolment numbers collated by Portuguese universities – suggests that different phenomena are being measured, thus clouding our impressions. A study by Sin et al (2022), however, suggests that while growth in the recruitment of international students has continued at Portuguese universities, expansion has been at a much slower pace compared to the pre-pandemic years – a position consistent with our own perceptions. Given the lack of clarity, any quantitative overview of international student immobility during the pandemic is always going to be somewhat opaque, and incomplete, as this ignores the qualitative impacts arising from the disruption, including the erosion of value within the learning experience.

Research conducted with international students in Portugal during the early months of the pandemic revealed some of the structural faults that had opened up in their lives, partly as a result of objectively poor living situations and partly due to the more general feeling of isolation (see Cairns et al, 2021a, 2021b; Malet Calvo et al, 2021). This all painted a pretty grim picture in the spring of 2020, but later reports suggest fairly rapid adaptation and acclimatization to changes in living and studying conditions; basically, international students are remarkably resilient. Institutions also kept going reasonably well, continuing to support the students they were hosting and managing to recruit greater numbers, sometimes onto online platforms. While there does seem to have been a dip in regard to participation in credit mobility, the enrolment of overseas students has grown in prominence during the pandemic in Portugal, suggesting that a different logic drives these mobilities, making them relatively impervious to the impact of COVID-19.

FIVE

Maintaining Migration during a Pandemic

Having looked at the impact of the pandemic on the tourism industry and the mobility of international students, in this chapter we turn our attention towards labour migration. This change of emphasis may appear strange to some readers, with migration traditionally seen as separate from what are considered 'softer' forms of mobility. However, while the experience of moving to another country for employment purposes substantially differs from other forms of global circulation, all three of these mobilities depend on the existence of a fully functioning international travel infrastructure and relatively open national borders. We can, therefore, anticipate a certain amount of shared experience among people on the move, even if their experiences are fundamentally different in many other respects.

Another commonality might be the idea of expansionism, discussed previously. As with tourism and student mobility, in the years preceding the onset of the pandemic, levels of labour migration to Portugal appeared to have increased, though not reaching the same levels recorded in other European countries. Residents with a foreign nationality represented around 5.7 per cent of the population residing in Portugal in 2019, rising to 6.4 per cent in 2020 (Oliveria, 2022). This represents a major contrast with, for example, Luxembourg, which had an equivalent figure of 47.4 per cent, and Malta, with 20.1 per cent (Monteiro and Oliveira, 2021). The actual size of the foreign population in Portugal is, however, a difficult issue to assess due to ambiguities within recording systems, although we can say that there has been a growth in the visibility of foreign workers. Also prominent in our evidence are signs of what might be termed 'periodic migration', with people travelling to Portugal repeatedly, but for relatively short stays, coinciding with the times during which they were needed by certain sectors of the economy. We might, then, see this as another example of the fractional or fluid migration we discussed in Chapter 4. But again, due to a lack of adequate statistics, we do not really have a precise idea of the scale of such circuitous practices.

Equally difficult to estimate is the exact contribution to the national economy made by labour migrants, although we are aware of the value of these workers to strategically important sectors, including agriculture. Public discourse on migration in Portugal also recognizes the contribution made by these workers to social security, and this is reflected in relevant statistics. Foreigners constitute a much higher proportion of contributors (64 per cent) than Portuguese nationals (45 per cent), and a lower proportion of social security beneficiaries (52 per cent) compared to nationals (83 per cent) (Monteiro and Oliveira, 2021). Despite the greater activation of social protection mechanisms during the pandemic, these disparities have largely been maintained, albeit with a slightly smaller differential between the two groups (Oliveria, 2022). We can, then, say that labour migrants are not regarded as constituting a burden on the state, and this helps explain why their presence has been traditionally seen as unproblematic by the public.

Labour migration and the pandemic

Provisionally, we can say that during the first year of the pandemic, the scale of migration to Portugal seems to have decreased, although we will have to wait until the publication of a full range of statistics before we can confirm this impression. But as we discuss later in this chapter, such figures will not necessarily take into account regional and micro-level variations, especially differences between urban and rural districts, nor do they recognize the dependence of certain sectors of the economy, such as agriculture, on migrant labour. Further confusing this picture is the important issue of internal or interregional migration taking place within the national territory. This includes the movement of labour migrants who lost their jobs in one region at the start of the pandemic and then moved within Portugal, and often between labour market sectors, towards the industries that had managed to remain more or less fully operational, a practice also noted in other European contexts at this time (see, for example, González-Leonardo et al, 2022; Stawarz et al, 2022). The need to circulate at the height of the pandemic nonetheless created problems for these migrants and introduced challenges for employers and local authorities, the latter charged with maintaining public health and, at the same time, keeping open what were deemed the most essential migration pathways.

This situation is also reflected at a national political level. On the whole, Portugal sought to maintain distance from processes that could be seen as strengthening nationalist or far right agendas. This included securing borders, with any closures framed as the erection of defensive barriers to stop the spread of the virus (Carlà, 2022; Dalingwater et al, 2022; Erayman and Çağlar, 2022). Attempts to maintain migration were also articulated by the authorities using humanitarian language (see Gorjão, 2020), but as our evidence shows, economic imperatives also persisted, reminding us of the potential profits at stake. This explains why attempts to maintain labour migration were grounded in financial concerns, echoing some of the discussion in Chapter 3 regarding tourism industry discourse at this time. The authorities also made reference to Portugal's economic vulnerabilities, given the country's relatively recent history of financial crisis, as well as the obvious need to feed the population.

While not overtly nationalistic, this debate still generated a clash of economic and epidemiological imperatives, creating tension in policymaking and rendering visible some previously under-represented or ignored issues relating to labour migration. The debate had potential, then, to alter the positive perception of migrant workers. When problems became visible, there was a risk of increasing far right politicians' opposition to labour migration. These politicians had previously focused their ire on other groups, referring to alleged insanitary living conditions, most prominently, among the Roma population, as has happened in other international contexts (see especially, Erayman and Çağlar, 2022). This suggests that the problematization of mobility during the pandemic in Portugal has social, cultural and political consequences as well as the more obvious economic and existential ones.

The immediate response

In regard to what actually happened during the early months of the pandemic, while many countries in Europe called for regularization programmes for migrant workers (PICUM, 2020), on 27 March 2020, less than ten days after the declaration of a national state of emergency in Portugal, some undocumented groups of workers were granted time-limited residence permits. It would seem that mobilization among some civil society organizations, concerned about the situation facing labour migrants as the pandemic started, contributed to the issuing of Order 3863-B/2020. With it, the Portuguese government acknowledged the need for temporary regularization of migrants who had made residence applications to the national migration and borders body, SEF; this enabled them to access the labour market as well as health care and certain welfare provisions. However, civil society organizations and academic scholarship soon began to highlight the limits of this initiative in terms of its temporary nature and limited target group (Wallis, 2020; Mazzilli, 2022).

Alongside the need to maintain labour migration during the pandemic and, with it, guarantee the ability to pass through internal and external borders, is the challenge of effectively managing the living and working conditions of migrant workers. This extends to becoming aware of the complications surrounding their journeys to and stays within a country that has temporarily suspended most of its international travel links and adopted a new discourse about the need to restrict practically all forms of population circulation, making migration ethically suspect. We can view this situation as another example of flux in the moral economy of mobility, with workers and employers, and perhaps some politicians, together giving labour migration exceptional status (this harks back to issues addressed in Chapter 2; see also Thompson, 1963, 1971). Nevertheless, maintaining migration had unforeseen consequences, with the public scrutiny of this exception making visible the objectively poor housing conditions endured by many of these migrants and creating the need for interventions to ensure compliance with health regulations during the migrants' seasonal stays in Portugal. We might, from a humanitarian point of view, see this as a positive outcome, albeit referring to a situation that should not have arisen in the first place.

To explore this issue further in this chapter, we focus on what has been described in Portugal as the 'Odemira case' and the broader issue of migration linked to agribusiness in Portugal, the latter being an issue that has attracted much attention in previous studies (Carvalho, 2021; Fonseca et al, 2021; Pereira et al, 2021; see also Esteves et al, 2017; Taboadela et al, 2018). For now, we can say that Odemira is a municipality in the southwestern Alentejo region, in which agriculture is both a major employer and a wealth generator, with the local economy highly reliant on seasonal migrants from outside the EU and some of these migrants continued to work and move within Portugal during periods of mandated immobility.

Labour migration in the pre-pandemic era

In regard to the issue of labour migration, we focus on Portugal as a destination for workers rather than an exit point. It is important to acknowledge this emphasis as it challenges the traditional view of the country as a place of outward migration. Certainly, in terms of academic studies, most past work has concentrated on 'emigration' rather than 'immigration', and perhaps still does, and this is also a view strongly re-enforced by public interest in diaspora communities abroad, including an annual celebration day for emigrants; this is named after Portugal's most renowned writer, Luís de Camôes, and celebrated each year on 10 June, the anniversary of the author's death. Taking a more balanced view, we might regard Portugal as having a mixed migration model, involving population flows in different directions, temporary and permanent migrants, and highly skilled workers alongside manual labourers (Peixoto, 2007).

In explaining the apparent dramatic change in the country's migration landscape, we can take note of a range of developments, but fundamental to understanding how Portugal became a sending and receiving country of labour migrants is the ascension, in 1986, of the country to the European political community that evolved into the EU. Joining this transnational entity meant taking on new norms and values in regard to geographical mobility, which in time evolved into a strong orientation towards free movement and circulation between national territories, including the diversification and multiplication of various forms of migration. Becoming part of the eventual EU meant more opportunities for Portuguese workers to move abroad, to countries including France, Germany and the UK; but it also enabled foreigners from fellow member states to enter Portugal, including workers from some Eastern European countries. These labour migrants complemented those who were following existing migration routes, especially from Brazil and the Portuguese-speaking countries in Africa. Together, these trends seem to have shaped labour migration in Portugal during the late 20th century and early 21st century, and contributed towards its cities becoming multicultural environments (Corkill and Eaton, 1998; Pires et al, 2010).

At a material level, we can also say that incoming labour migrants became economically important in Portugal, with fluctuations in levels of incoming migration associated with the health of the country's labour market (Pires, 2019); for instance, the country became less attractive as a destination during the years of austerity that followed the 2008 economic crisis, particularly as there were fewer job opportunities, but it became more appealing during the subsequent recovery period. These trends are broadly reflected in statistics published in national and international databases, including Eurostat and Pordata, the latter of which provides breakdowns on demographic change in the foreign population in Portugal, for citizens with legal resident status (Figure 5.1).

Figure 5.1: Foreign population with legal resident status, 1960–2020

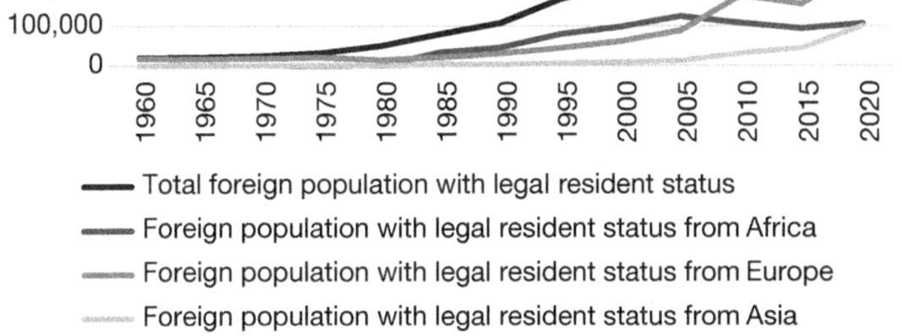

Source: Pordata, 'População estrangeira com estatuto legal de residente: total e por algumas nacionalidades' [Foreign population with legal resident status: total and by some nationalities] [online], Available from: www.pordata.pt/Portugal/População+estrangeira+com+estatuto+legal+de+residente+total+e+por+algumas+nacionalidades-24-184436 [accessed 1 May 2022]

Interesting to note in Figure 5.1 are the countries of origin of the more recent arrivals. This data suggests that new arrivals in Portugal are mostly from Asia, marking a contrast with the traditional picture of labour migrants being from other Portuguese-speaking countries, such as Angola, Brazil, Cape Verde and Mozambique. These individuals may have been attracted by the demand for labour in the agriculture sector, a development that is in itself related to investment in more intensive forms of farming, especially in rural areas in the south of the country, leading to an economic, social and demographic 'reconfiguration' of these regions (Fonseca et al, 2021). The suggestion is that labour migration, particularly the recruitment of short-term low-paid workers from overseas, is a potential driver of the economy in such areas, in contrast to other forms of migration, such as that of international students and highly skilled workers, which tends to be much more of an urban phenomenon, centred on the cities of Lisbon and Porto (see Chapter 4; see also Cairns et al, 2017).

An outstanding example of this 'new' migration to rural regions can be found in the municipality of Odemira in the Alentejo region. Located just over ten kilometres off the Atlantic coast, and close to the Costa Vicentina nature park, it is an area renowned for its agriculture, including forestry and livestock, as well as tourism and culture, with the village of Zambujeira do Mar hosting the annual Sudoeste festival, one of the largest rock festivals in Europe. Since the 1980s, the agribusiness sector in Odemira has recruited seasonal workers from abroad due to their flexibility and low cost, as has been the case in other regions of Portugal (Esteves et al, 2017). While not homogenous in terms of national backgrounds, in the past, most of these workers travelled from Eastern European countries, but more recently, there has been a major influx from Asia. We should also mention that the owners of some of these agribusinesses are also foreign, albeit from Northern European countries and conforming more to the norms of lifestyle migrants than those of labour migrants (Taboadela et al,

2018; Fonseca et al, 2021). This means that the Odemira case can be seen an example of a multifaceted migration process, illustrating the different ways in which the circulation of people and capital expanded in the pre-pandemic epoch.

In regard to the size of the migrant population in the municipality of Odemira, figures presented in Figure 5.2 suggest that this phenomenon has expanded considerably since 2008, especially in the years immediately prior to the pandemic, to the point of constituting a major demographic change in an area that was previously characterized by an ageing population and a low birth rate. This confirms that we are looking at a significant socio-demographic shift, reflecting the growth of agribusiness in the region at this time.

A growing foreign population in a municipality that is in demographic decline implies that the potential dynamism of the former can compensate for the dependency on social security of the latter in addition to meeting the needs of the

Figure 5.2: Foreign population with legal resident status in the municipality of Odemira, 2008–20

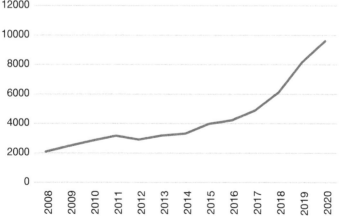

Source: SEF, 'População Estrangeira Residente em Portugal' [Foreign population resident in Portugal] [online], Available from: https://sefstat.sef.pt/forms/distritos. aspx\ [accessed 1 May 2022]

local labour market. This seems like a win-win situation, benefiting local businesses and the state as well as incoming labour migrants. Furthermore, the presence of these workers has not raised social unrest. In recent years, the category of 'migrant' has not attracted the same degree of pejorative usage in Portugal compared to what appears to have happened in other European countries.

In understanding why labour migration has not been problematized in Odemira, we should remember that this is a location characterized by historically low levels of incoming migrants and the still-fresh memories of Portuguese emigratory experiences, which has helped mitigate against the development of the kind of xenophobia that has made migration a site for proxy political wars elsewhere in the world (see also Koopmans and Statham, 2000; Erayman and Çağlar, 2022), as suggested by recent scholarship in France, Sweden and the UK (Dalingwater et al, 2022). Portugal's mainstream political parties, including the ruling Socialist Party (Partido Socialista) and the main opposition the Social Democratic Party (Partido Social Democrata), have tended to share a relatively positive view of labour migration (Carvalho and Duarte, 2020), and while there have been concerns regarding the behaviour of certain individuals employed by SEF, in recent years, documented incidents of violence against migrants have attracted censure rather than sympathy for the agency.[1]

Despite this relatively positive atmosphere, many seasonal migrant workers still face practical problems, as do other migrants and Portuguese citizens who lack access to social and economic capital, with additional concerns about the process of regularizing their stays, including gaining access to local welfare services and finding appropriate housing.[2] The practical problems facing labour migrants appear to be particularly acute in areas like Odemira, with housing a particular concern in the municipality. It is not hard to see why. An expanded foreign population in the region has led to significant increases in the value of properties; prices, according to one recent study, have grown more rapidly than the national average, contributing to reduced access to decent housing conditions for modestly paid workers (Fonseca et al, 2021). This issue was recognized before the start of the pandemic, and the need to respond to the challenges posed by a lack of access to decent housing and the wider integration of the migrant population into Portuguese society has prompted the mobilization of a broad spectrum of actors and various ad hoc interventions and structures (see also Comissão Municipal do Imigrante, 2015, 2019, 2020). Among these structures is the Local Support Centre for the Integration of Migrants (Centro Local de Apoio à Integração de Migrantes), which has been in operation in Odemira since 2016, partly funded by the local municipality.

In regard to why such centres are needed, we can interpret the new wave of labour migration to Portugal as another form of mobility expansionism that, as with tourism, appears to have taken place without sufficient preparation or adaptation, with corporate considerations overriding humanitarian concerns. The political power of agribusiness enterprises in fact led to the creation of a 'special and transitional regime', which authorized the placement of migrant workers in precarious housing on local farms (Presidência do Conselho de Ministros, 2019). These residences are, in bureaucratic language, Removable Temporary Accommodation Facilities (Instalações de Alojamento Temporário Amovíveis), known in common parlance as containers (*contentores*). Described by government actors as 'worthy' housing and 'temporary' practical responses, they have received strong criticism, including allegations of a lack of political accountability and human rights violations arising from increased exposure to labour exploitation and few opportunities for integration among the workers. In addition, this measure does not address the lack of actual housing for most migrant workers, who frequently end up crammed together in dwellings that lack the facilities needed to maintain an adequate standard of living (see also Fonseca et al, 2021).

Labour migration in the pandemic era

Moving towards the present, we look now at the impact of successive waves of COVID-19 in regions like Odemira, having noted possible concerns with labour migrants' living conditions and the potential difficulty they might have in adhering to pandemic protocols in what can be extremely cramped housing. In normal circumstances, potentially unsanitary conditions, including overcrowding and lack of access to basic facilities, would be a concern, but this became an even bigger issue at times when social distancing was mandatory.

Equally concerning was the risk that the perception of labour migration would shift as an outcome of the high level of publicity surrounding the situation, with a move from perceiving migration as a relatively benign or even positive force towards seeing the presence of significant numbers of foreign nationals as a problem. This was even more of an issue when workers travelled to Portugal at times when international and internal travel was actively discouraged, creating the impression that these workers were selfishly ignoring the public health guidelines and becoming potential vectors of virus transmission. We might say then that the expansion of labour migration followed by an unanticipated pandemic has implications for migration narratives in Portugal, the labour migrants themselves and other Portuguese residents concerned about contracting COVID-19.

This is a debate we return to, on a theoretical level, in the next chapter, but for now we want to look at some of the practical measures that were taken to manage this situation, drawing on insights from empirical research conducted in first half of 2022. In regard to research subjects, interviews were conducted with experts in the migration field, all of whom had direct knowledge of the Odemira situation, being representatives of relevant government departments and civil society agencies in Portugal.

One important finding of our research confirms the position, asserted earlier, that labour migration has not – until now – been seen as a major problem by local politicians in Portugal, or by the public, and that the positive contribution migrants make to society is generally recognized. This was certainly the view of one representative of a government agency working in the migration field, who confirmed that the positive view of labour migrants extends to the very top of the Portuguese political establishment:

'In Portugal we need migrants. Migrants contribute to social security. Most of the migrant population in Portugal is active, and we need more migrants to work. The Prime Minister and the President of the Republic want migrants to be treated as well in Portugal as the Portuguese abroad, and therefore we have this progressive attitude.'

This view on labour migration can be considered a hegemonic position, shared by the main political parties in Portugal, regardless of their ideological differences, although this obviously does not extend to the much smaller far right parties. From this account, we can also see that this is not a position grounded in sentimentality or even humanitarian concerns. It is, rather, a pragmatic acknowledgment of the social and economic importance of labour migrants and the contribution they make to Portuguese society. This is, then, a nice summation of the position that has helped prevent migration from becoming a site of cultural and political conflict, since inviting foreign workers to Portugal is seen as a way of filling the state coffers as well as benefiting migrants themselves, whether they are labourers, entrepreneurs, students or lifestyle-oriented travellers. If we are being more candid, we might also admit that such positivity is needed in order to attract migrants to Portugal, given the country's relatively remote geopolitical position, far from the European centre, and with an economic profile that is seen as less attractive than that of other countries, even neighbouring Spain. As well as being pragmatic, this position reflects a remarkable degree of maturity at official level, and a refreshing contrast to the unimaginative, tired and often racist discourse that has become part of mainstream politics in so many countries.

The geographical and economic marginality of Portugal also seems to deter potentially irregular entrants from entering the country. For example, the kind of small boat crossings from North Africa, seen as a problem in neighbouring Spain and in Italy, are rare in Portugal. On the few occasions when people do arrive by such means, their presence creates confusion rather than hostility, and it is assumed that they have made a navigation error and their intended destination was somewhere else. This situation was noted by a representative of a non-governmental organization (NGO), making reference to one such event that took place during the pandemic period:

'Portugal is not a direct port for [irregular] migrants, even if there was a recent exception when a hundred migrants from Morocco landed in the Algarve region. This created some excitement. It seemed that we were starting to be invaded, but many of them had barely arrived when they fled to Spain. Even if they were earning less money here, they could have had some stability due to the lack of manpower in certain economic sectors, such as agriculture, construction and fishing, which, due to difficult working conditions, are not popular with Portuguese workers. They also had the prospect of seeing their situations regularized, but they already had families in Spain.'

The view that Portugal is not the preferred destination for migrants (regular or otherwise) was further re-enforced by another interviewee, who emphasized that 'they are here today, a month or two and then they are gone. They go to other countries because Portugal is not an attractive country, not even for the Portuguese, let alone for migrants.' Looking at this position from a slightly different point of view, it might also be argued that incoming migrants have more leverage in Portugal than they do in other countries due to their relative rarity,[3] and the dependency of Portugal on foreign workers also gives them a certain amount of political protection against being problematized, particularly considering the need for labour migration in crucial sectors such as agriculture. Even during the pandemic, farming had to remain operational so that the population could be fed, meaning that the flow of migrants had to continue even if risks to public health were generated.

This still left the challenge of ensuring that workers' stays could be safe and in compliance with the new public safety requirements at the time, which presented numerous practical obstacles. Housing was obviously important, but following public health protocols was not the only concern. Complications extended to the interruption of regularization processes due to the closure of SEF offices, with the pandemic deepening existing bureaucratic backlogs; this meant that migrants' paperwork could not be processed rapidly during the long periods of lockdown. Nevertheless, the government representative quoted earlier in the chapter stated:

'We took great care of those who stayed here with immobility, ensuring that they all had the same support during the pandemic as the rest of the people. As soon as the confinement started, after about a week, we knew that many migrants were not regularized – that is, they were waiting for regularization by SEF, and some had not even managed to submit their request. We immediately issued an order for the migrants who had submitted their requests to be considered as documented and given access to support the same as other Portuguese citizens.'

This may have been the aspiration, but the practical implementation of these policies seems to have been somewhat incomplete. Other interviewees, especially those with close proximity to the migrant workers, recognized the importance of these interventions but remained more critical of how the measures taken at this time were implemented, and of the procedures themselves. An NGO representative explained:

'The government say that this measure allows access to all public services, but this is not the case. The first thing it allowed was the issue of the health service user number. It is not a mandatory number, but without it there is a risk of paying more at the time of a consultation, and you cannot have a family doctor, assuming you can find one. It gives access to social benefits, to the unemployment subsidy. However, migrants contribute more than they receive, and it is rare that they ask for a subsidy of unemployment as they just look for another job.'

This debate over the issue of regularization opens up further questions regarding labour migrants' status within Portugal and the extent to which foreign workers are actually being treated the same as Portuguese citizens. As another interviewee, also an NGO representative, added:

'The government has regularized the "permanence" in Portugal of all migrants. Permanence does not mean [a] residence permit, but it helps people to access services, albeit on a temporary basis. It was a matter of public health, of social emergency, and it was necessary to take these measures, as … people were scared. They had emotional needs and required answers to questions that were not translated into foreign languages. People came here looking for it, taking up the whole block. There were people who came from catering – one of the most affected sectors [as] even when the restaurants reopened, they were empty – who found work in agriculture. There were also workers who went to Europe in search of work. People don't stand still. When migrants don't have work, they go looking for work, even outside the borders. There were people moving within the country and others leaving the country.'

We can see that positive political rhetoric does not mean managing problems on the ground is easy, and in fact many practical challenges remain. It is clear from this account that there was a shift in migration patterns due to migrants who had lost their jobs in one place needing to move to another were their labour was still required. This situation created the need to maintain circulation within the country at a time of mandated immobility between and within regions. Therefore, more conspicuous exceptions had to be made to accommodate the wishes of these migrants, especially where there was an alignment between their immediate needs and economic imperatives in areas such as agriculture.

The case of Odemira

We turn again to the Odemira case, but from the vantage point of one year later, in the spring of 2022, when academic studies engaging with this topic have started to emerge, some of which acknowledge the interaction between immobility in the pandemic and pre-existing problems (see, for example, Mazzilli, 2022). As already noted, to analyse the values and norms that guided interventions at the moment of crisis, and the broader question of how to manage labour migration before, during and after an unprecedented time of immobility, we entered into dialogue with stakeholders in the migration field in Portugal. With the help of these individuals, we were able to explore the moral economy of this migration episode, acknowledging how the Odemira case affected our ways of thinking about forms of labour migration that were previously considered unproblematic and beneficial to the national economy, but which created a new range of social obligations.

Out of this fieldwork, we can see that the pandemic rapidly changed both the lives of many labour migrants and the public perception of various non-essential forms of mobility. In addition, there were practical problems affecting how people worked and lived during this time. As noted in the previous section, many people employed in sectors such as hospitality suddenly lost their jobs and had to find alternative employment in other occupations. This required them to move from one region to another in Portugal while the pandemic lockdowns were in force: from the closed-down cities to rural regions were labour was still required in agriculture. In regard to those who moved to Odemira, according to some local interviewees, agricultural enterprises, along with local authorities, now had the task of managing the new influx of migrants and securing their living conditions, with unexpected costs and complications:

> 'Agricultural companies were the only companies that did not stop during the pandemic. But in order not to stop working, they had to take some measures to avoid having outbreaks ... mass testing – workers were all tested twice a week, for example. This increased costs. If we had to reinvent ourselves in order to stay connected and help migrants – for example, by video calls – companies had to do the same. They had to reorganize all their work so that work teams would not cross paths in the fields, in cafeterias, on transport. They had to change their own organization inside the container.'

Despite efforts to keep labour migration operational in Portugal, we can see that some practical, and possibly political, problems remained. Not only did workers have to cope with poor working conditions, but their highly visible presence in the country came at time when all forms of non-essential mobility were discouraged, risking inflaming the kind of anti-migrant sentiment that has spread within many other European countries. These inconsistencies were noted by an NGO representative who had experience of interventions related to employment of migrant workers in the agricultural sector and an awareness of the health risks associated with their mobility during the pandemic:

'The internal mobility of migrant workers remained high, even if they had not entered from outside the country. The first migrants to show up with COVID in the Algarve region, in Tavira, left Serpa in March and arrived in Tavira in April. They were the first 20 to be confined that I had news of. Then, in Odemira, an Indian who had come from Lisbon infected all the people in the house where he lived, 20 or so, and the place where he worked. We immediately advised that it was not the migrants who were the problem. The situation, namely the degraded housing conditions, the large number of people sleeping in a room or a house, already existed. Migrants were a risk group. It wasn't because they were Asians or Africans, but because of their living situation.'

These insights confirm the idea that since the start of the pandemic, different factors have converged to complicate labour migration in Portugal, putting working migrants and those they are in close contact with at risk. Importantly, it is not the migrants who are seen as the problem but rather their unsuitable living conditions, particularly in the more intensive periods of lockdown and at the start of the pandemic, when there was a lack of knowledge about how to control the spread of COVID-19. Nevertheless, an association has been made between migrants and the virus, threatening the integrity of the positive narrative on labour migration in Portugal and necessitating interventions to maintain the country's attractiveness for migrant workers.

The moral economy of pandemic mobility

In this section, we return to the idea of moral economy and the ability of strategic alliances to redefine societal norms – in this case, the apparent alignment between labour migrants, their employers and state authorities in Portugal, with a view to maintaining open labour migration pathways. This scenario is obviously quite different from the historical struggles of the English peasantry described by E.P. Thompson, or even the alliance of holidaymakers and tourism industry suggested in Chapter 3, but it is no less interesting and represents an important aspect of the immobility turn that recognizes change in migration discourses.

We might hypothesize that allowing labour migration to continue led to a clash of competing imperatives, with the importance of the work to be undertaken by agricultural workers enabling migration pathways to remain open at a time when many other forms of travel were discouraged. What seems to have been under-appreciated are the practical issues – most prominently, the need to adequately house these migrants, as their precarious living conditions made the process of complying with health and safety strictures extremely difficult. Furthermore, that the special dispensation granted to labour migrants was not effectively managed started to bring into question the idea that labour migration was a positive force in Portugal, since it was now being reported as a problem, becoming a staple of the news cycle in Portugal in the spring of 2021. The surge in COVID-19 infections in the municipality of Odemira sparked heated debate and brought to light these precarious living conditions. If there was a silver lining in this dark cloud for migrant workers in the agricultural sector it was the fact that their problems became a focus for interventions from the state and various enterprises. In fact, some of the workers ended up being housed by government authorities, first in the gymnasium of a school in São Teotónio and then in a private eco holiday resort on the Costa Vicentina, to enable them to socially isolate.

This was obviously not the end of the matter, with consternation generated within the region by agriculture and local tourism, who did not welcome the extra expense and perceived financial damage to their properties. The civil requisition of the Zmar Eco Experience resort also raised complaints among property owners, although the enterprise had been closed to the public at this time and some compensation was eventually provided. More tellingly, as one of our interviewees from a relevant NGO stated: 'Odemira only made the news because it appeared on television, but the country is full of Odemiras.' The implication is that this was not a unique case, and Portugal is obviously not the only country with precarious and marginalized migrant workers, giving this debate wider resonance.

To address the issue, in the period following the publicizing of this emergency, the Portuguese government intervened further, with a new resolution issued by the Council of Ministers to request state support for the placement of new containers near the workers' greenhouses. The local council in Odemira has also been active at this time, with existing and new initiatives in relation to housing; as another interviewee explained:

'Since the end of 2019, we have started working with the council of Odemira. It still did not have a local housing strategy, which was the main measure to obtain financing for decent housing. At the same time, there was the resolution of the Council of Ministers for the installation of temporary accommodation, which was not being implemented. … What was achieved in 2021 is that the council finally presented the local housing strategy and there was a new resolution by the Council of Ministers so that in addition to the installation of temporary accommodation, there could be other strategies, such as renting houses in Alentejo, half an hour away, in an empty village. For this, you need transport – either from the council or from the company.'

At the time of conducting our research, the formation of a migrant organization in Odemira was also reported by government interviewees. This opened up the prospect of further change in migration management, suggesting more participation from migrants themselves in regard to improving their living conditions. For now, we can say that this complicated situation points to a new range of factors that seriously affect the meaning of various mobilities, including labour migration, initiating an apparent conflict between established norms and the attempt to enforce a new mobility etiquette to control the spread of the virus. We come back to this issue in the next chapter.

Summary

The Odemira case was a complicated situation, and the pandemic clearly made labour migration more convoluted, while also confirming its importance for Portugal. But harking back to some of the theoretical ideas relating to moral economy explored in Chapter 2, the impression is that at a time when there had been a major redefinition of mobility norms, aimed at effectively suspending internal and international migration, the new 'rules' were upended to serve the needs of agribusiness and, by association, migrant workers, and ultimately the state, constituting an alliance of interest groups. Together, these forces were able, as the title of this chapter suggests, to maintain migration within Portugal, albeit not without generating a new range of problems in relation to the image and the reality of labour migration.

It is also important when discussing these matters at a theoretical level to remind ourselves of the human impact of these machinations. We have observed in this chapter that labour migrants – people who want to make a living and who are also making a vital contribution to the agriculture industry – were placed in unsanitary conditions and were then subject to intrusive media scrutiny at a time when they were under considerable stress due to the epidemiological situation and their own pre-existing precarious economic positions. This has been the reality of labour migration during the pandemic for thousands of people in Portugal and millions more worldwide. Therefore, when we talk about an 'immobility turn', we should remember that this is more than a temporary interruption in tourism or the placing on hold of ambitions to study abroad – it also involves the heightening of tensions among a section of the population who deserve recognition for their efforts at this time, in making a valuable contribution to society.

SIX

Mobility after an Immobility Turn

In the final chapter of this book, we return to debates about the meaning of mobility and how this changed after the freedom to move was suspended for long periods during the first two years of the COVID-19 pandemic. This discussion acknowledges social, economic and political imperatives that possess the power to open and close mobility pathways and the pursuit of sustainability in regard to balancing the positive and negative impacts of expanded levels of international travel. While determining an optimal level of circulation has always been difficult, the pandemic further complicated this process, extending to a need to work out how to keep mobility profitable while maintaining public safety.

To make sense of this situation, we return to the conceptual ideas introduced in the preceding chapters. In Chapters 1 and 2, we looked at the mobility turn and the multiplication of mobilities that took place over the course of several decades, most intensively during the 1990s and the early years of the 21st century. This prolonged period of expansion led to maximized levels of human circulation in multiple forms, especially but not exclusively in international tourism. In these two chapters, we acknowledged not only the importance of prior theoretical developments on this theme but also what seems to have been a largely unheeded critique of expansionism, something that could not continue indefinitely due to sustainability concerns. We will never know how the mobility turn would have ultimately played out, since the pandemic meant expansionism never quite reached its apogee, but the diffusion of mobilities attained was still extremely impressive in quantitative terms, even if the quality of the experiences often left a lot to be desired.

As implied in Chapter 3, another problem that emerged during the period of expansionism was the unregulated and/or mismanaged development of mobilities, resulting in multiple forms of extractivism taking place and removing the meaningfulness of much travel through saturating host communities with over-entitled – and often annoying – visitors, creating an intensified variant of the 'tourist gaze' (Urry and Larsen, 2011). The mobilities looked at in Chapters 4 and 5, meanwhile, appear to illustrate less problematic forms of expansionism, which were, nevertheless, not entirely benign due to concerns regarding social inclusivity in student mobility and problems with supporting labour migrants, particularly at times of heightened stress, like the lockdown periods during the pandemic. What we can deduce is that societies need to take better care of their migrants and recognize that being a host involves taking on costs as well as reaping the benefits. This realization leaves us to ponder what will happen next, after the immobility turn. The discussion in this chapter does not make predictions or draw conclusions in the traditional sense of reaching a point of closure, since the pandemic itself has not come to a neat and tidy ending, but we have identified a number of insights to help us understand what might happen after the period of flux has settled down.

(Im)mobility in flux

The first of these concerns relates to the meaning of mobility, or rather the discourses on mobility that underpin these meanings, and the persistence of inherently flawed narratives, including the idea that sustainability can be nested within expansionism. Alongside this point is the issue of unpredictability surrounding international travel, something that has continued after the lifting of sanitary measures, influenced by a wide range of factors, including industrial unrest and the invasion of Ukraine. At a micro level, we might also say that the meaning of migration is subject to change according to the needs and wants of various actors, and this may happen in regard to other forms of non-essential mobility. Certainly, during the pandemic, there were very obvious shifts in meaning, from seeing international travel as a pleasure to realizing that it had become a bit of a pain. The moral economy perspective hypothesized in Chapter 2 also brings to light some of the processes that legitimate and de-legitimate the freedom to circulate, with hegemonic discourses defining not only what is practically possible but also what can be considered societally acceptable. Using a Foucauldian framework, we argue that a temporary shift took place in mobility discourse, at least during the first year of the pandemic, but this change was temporary and unstable, and was dispensed with rapidly and perhaps prematurely, meaning that the expectations of many travellers could not be realistically met after the attempted reopening of societies in the spring of 2022.

A second, more straightforward insight relates to a change of emphasis in the marketing of mobility, including the integration of sustainability discourse into international tourism. It is hard to ignore the fact that much pre-pandemic mobility was inherently unsustainable, given the problems generated in the most popular destinations by alleged overtourism (see Chapter 3), and while an extractivist ethos may remain hegemonic in some corners of the tourism industry, the idea that more tourists is an always a good thing is at least being challenged. Given the importance of marketing to our understanding of tourism, it is interesting that the industry itself is rethinking its ideas, or at least trying to offer visitors something different, including the rediscovery of 'digital nomadism'.

Mobility discourses

Among the public, reactions to immobility during the pandemic obviously varied, with some people lamenting the loss of their entitlements more than others. Alongside nostalgia for the freedom to engage in relatively carefree travel, there was also relief at the end of unpopular commutes and pointless business trips. These issues are hard to quantify, but if we are being honest with ourselves, we might admit that while a holiday could be nice in theory, the reality was often much different. International travel was, in fact, often arduous and uncomfortable, and that was long before it became a vector of potentially deadly virus transmission. And of course, not everyone could afford to travel, or to travel as frequently or as far as they would have liked. It therefore seems rather odd to completely forget about all of the old inconveniences and limitations, not to mention the huge carbon footprint that was being generated by aviation, and remember only the good times that did not actually exist for many people.

In trying to explain why a generally positive view of mobility has persisted, especially in regard to international tourism, certain pre-pandemic ideas seem to have survived the ravages of two years of disruption and disappointment. This is despite the fact that concerted state-endorsed efforts were made, especially during the early stages of the public health crisis, to convince people that practically all of their mobility was unnecessary – or 'non-essential', to use the jargon deployed at the time – and could, therefore, be easily dispensed with. At the same time, when circulation was permitted, the international travel experience was problematized as part of the efforts to limit the spread of COVID-19, with the establishment of a new mobility etiquette, including the observation of uncomfortable and inconvenient regulations. This move can of course be seen as a corollary of the more general pandemic-era discourse on public health, aimed at reorienting human behaviour away from convivial activities and towards pragmatic insularity, the rationale for doing so being grounded in medical science. The strength of pre-pandemic mobility narratives, however, meant that change was always going to be resisted and hard to sustain, and that two discourses about international travel would be co-existing with each other rather than one displacing the other.

From a sociological point of view, in referring to discourses, we should say that we mean bodies of ideas that define acceptable and unacceptable behaviour. More specifically, the mobility discourse of the pandemic has been comprised of ideas, images and narratives as well as formal edicts issued by the state. We are then recognizing the importance of the messages that circulate to regulate the behaviour of the public, including mobile subjects. Acknowledging the presence of this discursive formation enables us to make comparisons with how theorists such as Michel Foucault sought to explain different facets of human behaviour – for example, the regulation of human sexuality through attempts at repression or the desire to control criminals in carceral settings via panoptical observation (see Foucault, 1990, 1991). Those scenarios are not quite the same as the attempt to curb various forms of mobility, but share a subtlety that might be described in simpler terms as a form of imaginative discipline. Another important point to note is that the exercise of discursive power does not need to be coercive, except perhaps in exceptional cases where people are very visibly breaking the 'law'. What is crucial is the creation of the impression that the suggested behaviours are what everyone else is doing – regardless of whether or not this is the case – and to act otherwise would be seen as some kind of an unthinkable faux pas.

In summarizing this approach, during the pandemic attempts were made to exercise power in a nuanced manner with a view to turning people away from travelling. Norms were established for how one should, and shouldn't, behave, and the existence of these *regulations* was made evident through visible examples, including health and safety publicity campaigns and online notices regarding the present state of COVID-19 restrictions, extending to advice published on tourism industry websites. There were also implied rewards for those who conformed to the new orthodoxy and implied sanctions that were to be levied against others who refused to help reify the episteme. Examples of 'good behaviour' were fairly easy to identify – people staying at home and not travelling – but as we come to discuss, the disciplining of those who appeared to break the rules was less stringent. In regard to the authority of the new mobility discourse, of fundamental importance was the place of scientific knowledge, and the granting of authority to recognized experts in the health field, personages who also needed to be made visible. This explains why public health experts, who had previously occupied a marginal position in policymaking, suddenly became the centrepieces of nightly news broadcasts and associated media, their presence confirming that politicians had momentarily ceded power to a higher authority.

In evaluating the success of the new episteme, there appears to have been a high level of adherence to the new order during the first wave of infections; for example, the statistics explored in Chapter 1 suggest fairly uniform acceptance of the request to avoid non-essential travel. However, we also know from the research presented in Chapters 4 and 5 that certain forms of migration successfully evaded the restrictions after this point in time, in some cases for understandable reasons. After the first few months of the pandemic, students started to arrive again and international tourism also resumed, albeit in a constricted manner. This picture of partial adherence suggests a failure of the new mobility discourse to become hegemonic, or that it was never intended to become established, and that the ceding of authority to regulate mobility to 'science' was deliberately ineffective. We can also argue that enforcement of sanctions against unnecessary travel was inconsistent, with many blind eyes turned, especially when there was political capital to be gained from making exceptions.

The most egregious examples of the effacement of mobility etiquette in the Portuguese context were, arguably, the overturning of national norms by international imperatives and the machinations of an authority capable of making its own laws – namely, the Union of European Football Associations, commonly known as UEFA. A notorious case was the hosting of the 2021 men's Champions League football final in the city of Porto. The original plan was to contain thousands of visiting supporters of the finalists, Chelsea and Manchester City, in protective environments, separate from the city's citizens, a decision ratified by the Portuguese government, since the event took place when social gatherings were restricted, with professional football matches taking place without spectators.[1] This plan was soon abandoned, and invited guests of UEFA were given special dispensation to ignore sanitary measures. This created a bizarre situation, with the sense of transgression generated by the visitors' presence illustrating the tension created by there being two simultaneously existing mobility discourses, with the old order reasserting itself over the new narrative with ease. In more prosaic terms, the visiting supporters and dignitaries were allowed to do what Portuguese fans had not been allowed to in the 15 months before that: go to a football match. This must have been particularly galling for the fans of FC Porto, who were still not allowed to enter their own stadium. Furthermore, a number of the English-based fans overstayed, some engaging in antisocial behaviour, including attacks on police and members of the public in Porto. This is a very clear example of what goes wrong when the discursive 'law' is broken, leading to serious, even fatal, consequences, with the highly contagious Delta variant of COVID-19 spread from England to Portugal, creating another wave of infections.[2]

Sustainable mobilities

Finally, we want to consider the prospects for developing more sustainable modes of international travel. This is an issue we introduced in Chapter 3 with a brief exploration of some of the adaptations that had taken place in the marketing of tourism in Portugal, possibly in response to changing customer demands during the pandemic, to the point of making the pursuit of visitors' health and safety part of the marketing message. We might even say that certain aspects of pandemic mobility discourse were being intertwined with economic imperatives, including the desire of the tourism industry to remain operational at a time of limited possibilities. It also became evident in the analysis of our evidence from tourism stakeholders that such steps were still quite tentative and likely to have a limited appeal since peace and quiet is not what many people actually want during their holidays.

Given the prospect of increasing visitor numbers once more, the return of the old mobility narrative might complicate the challenge of making tourism sustainable. Part of the ease with which the familiar narratives are able to return relates to levels of prior investment and dependency on associated revenues. The sunk costs of tourism – jumbo-sized cruise ship terminals, the conversion of residential properties into short-term letting sites and the building of new airports – result in a reluctance on the part of private investors and the public sector to accept change that might dent their profits. A similar logic might be detected elsewhere. As implied in Chapter 4, the reliance of universities on income from overseas students is well known, with this revenue now helping to compensate for other funding shortfalls and potential losses incurred during the pandemic; attracting fee-paying student migrants hence becomes more important. Labour migrants, meanwhile, occupy a more ambiguous position, since they are, in theory, beneficiaries of mobility as well as income generators for their employers and contributors to the coffers of the receiving country. We might say, then, they have an importance that tourists do not possess, particularly in sectors where they are needed.

Focusing once again on tourism, the return of large numbers of tourists risks reigniting the processes that serve to extract value from host communities, or at least cause major disruption – something that may be less evident among migrants who are investing in these places and making a positive net contribution. There is also the issue of discomfort generated by intrusive visitors. Although there are extreme examples of tourists practically trampling cities like Venice to death, a more common experience has been the subjection of local residents to an uncomfortable 'tourist gaze' (Urry and Larsen, 2011), with the relationship between hosts and visitors becoming inherently non-reciprocal. This is likely to become even more alienating when some people, especially those with health conditions that make them vulnerable, are still adhering to what are no longer mandatory public health protocols, including mask wearing and social distancing, practices that many holidaymakers want nothing to do with. It will also be interesting to observe how an already-stretched public health service will cope with a re-influx of visitors at a time when there will be demands from exhausted employees to take time off for their own holidays. Similarly, it will be interesting to see how the return of visitors will be handled by the transportation sector, which has seen overheads rise and profit margins fall as a result of rising fuel prices following the invasion of Ukraine in February 2022. We might, then, say that the shift back to the old mobility patterns have their consequences, which need to be taken into account when we talk about a return to pre-pandemic levels of circulation.

Digital nomadism

These concerns suggest that restarting full-scale tourism in the middle, not the end, of a pandemic is going to invite a certain amount of chaos, with the potential for confusion to emerge following two years of atrophy and undercapacity in the industry, and a possible lack of preparation for the lifting of regulations. This situation might take us back towards thinking about the benefits that can be created for the environment and societies by fewer international flights and fewer visitors, with holidaymakers also able to take advantage of the relative emptiness of the less visited destinations.

These are fairly self-evident considerations, but we might also want to consider the viability of hybrid solutions to avoid chaos during the period of readjustment, perhaps making use of digital technology to support modes of travel that integrate tourism with labour migration, including a reactivation of the idea of digital nomadism. This is not a new approach to international travel, but it has grown in prominence during the pandemic. However, academic studies on digital nomadism appear to be scarce, focused mainly on the migration of the highly skilled and qualified (see, for example, Marques et al, 2021) and do not necessarily provide ringing endorsements of the approach due to the disruption to the sense of self while engaging in the practice (see, for example, Thompson, 2019; Green, 2020). We might, then, want to exercise a degree of caution and note that this is not an approach that will be suitable for all travellers.

The basic principle behind digital nomadism is, nevertheless, familiar and not necessarily problematic in itself. There is no consensus on who first coined the phrase (see Makimoto and Manners, 1997), but it is generally understood that a digital nomad is a person who is physically located in one space while technically employed in another, fulfilling work responsibilities remotely via the use of information technology. There is also a strong association with being situated in destinations associated with tourism, integrating work with leisure. We might say that the digital nomad is not quite a migrant but not a tourist either. This is why it is described as a hybrid form of circulation, using online and offline facilities. The rationale for 'digital nomadism' is also transversal, combining economic imperatives with lifestyle considerations – that is, using flexible working conditions to take advantage of a favourable local climate and more interesting cultural attractions, and perhaps lower taxation regimes. There is also variability in its formats. While it often involves dividing oneself between two or more countries, switching between urban and rural locations in the same country is another possibility; the latter creates fewer bureaucratic complications and offers a greater degree of cultural continuity.

Despite the paucity of research, the existing impression in our Portuguese context is that digital nomadism can be interpreted as an extension of lifestyle migration (see, for example, Torkington, 2012; Benson and O'Reilly, 2016), something that has traditionally been seen as a fairly elitist pursuit, indulged in by relatively small numbers of affluent individuals working in highly skilled, and highly flexible, professions. However, this position has changed profoundly with the pandemic and widespread practice of remote working in many different occupational fields, and we may yet see a reaction to the climate emergency involving greater numbers of people seeking working conditions that eliminate continuous commuting (see also Thompson, 2018). We might, then, want to rethink the constitution of the digital nomad population and move towards a slightly more inclusive view of this practice, taking into account the fact that environmentalism is already important to many people. More imaginatively, the format could conceivably be adapted to tertiary education; while students might still travel to another country, they do not necessarily need to spend all their time closely connected to a university campus and may even prefer to be based in another location if this suits their lifestyle needs. Where the approach would obviously fall down is in respect to the kind of labour migration practices we discussed in Chapter 5, since this work involves being grounded in a specific place in order to undertake essential manual work.

The idea is not without problems. Although marketed as flexible and carefree working, digital nomadism can be seen as an additional form of precarity and part of the globalization of a gig economy, especially when it is undertaken out of economic necessity rather than personal choice. We might even say that this has already happened during the periods of lockdown, when not everyone wanted or enjoyed being outside their traditional workplaces for long periods. It is also important to consider the challenges for service industries that depend on the presence of people in their factories, shops and offices, ranging from security staff to sandwich sellers. Clearly, the shift towards remote working will not suit all people and all occupations.

In reinventing digital nomadism, we would like to suggest two different formats that warrant future exploration, the first of which learns from the experience of working at home during the first two years of the pandemic. While for people living relatively close to their workplaces, this might have involved short-distance remote working, others took the opportunity to leave what might have been unsafe conditions and relocate to more peaceful and spacious locations, including urban-to-rural shifts. This may not be indicative of a lasting change, especially as remote working could have been an involuntary move. It would nevertheless be interesting to re-evaluate this episode as a potentially new form of digital nomadism, particularly in regard to any lasting effects. The second format relates to some of the ideas presented by the tourism industry in Portugal in Chapter 3, providing a more restricted form of nomadism that involves moving for extended periods to relatively remote locations with purpose-built or suitably adapted facilities. While this might be seen as an elitist activity or a new kind of working holiday, it is significant that such nomadism is both recognized by mainstream tourism agencies and aligned with sustainability goals. The pandemic 'experiment' suggests that there is a need to take a more in-depth look at inclusive and exclusive forms of digital nomadism available to 'regular' workers – not just elites – who want to work outside the traditional workplace without censure, suitably supported and equipped.

Summary

Bringing this book to a close, it is perhaps too early to determine whether there have been lasting changes in the meaning and materiality of mobilities after the first two years of the pandemic. If we are being optimistic, and there are no further major outbreaks of COVID-19, a lot of the problems and discomfort may soon be forgotten, and what we have termed the 'immobility turn' will be happily consigned to history. We might then conclude that the transformations that took place at this time, though substantial enough to have created instability across the mobility field, were not as serious as they might have been.

Despite this optimism, writing in the spring of 2022 we can say that we have not reached a point of recovery, although a great deal of progress is being made in regard to opening up societies to travellers once again. We might also say that we are witnessing a concerted effort to create the impression that it is business as usual for international travel, representing perhaps another discursive shift. It is, however, unfortunate that the moment was not anticipated or adequately prepared for, with insufficient staff at many airports to cater for the new wave of passengers, not to mention concerns about cost of living among aviation industry employees that may lead to strikes and other forms of industrial action. We might say that alongside implications arising from a long period of immobility and disrupted circulation, there will be problems created by the challenge of remobilization, which may continue to create difficulties for some time to come. We close then on a note of caution and with a reminder that patience and planning is still required by travellers, whether departing for long durations or short stays. We note also a certain amount of trepidation about the impact of the rising cost of living, especially increasing fuel and energy costs. While we are not suggesting that we will soon be experiencing another immobility turn on the same scale as that initiated by the pandemic, some individuals may be immobilized by having to use their economic resources for immediate concerns, such as eating, paying their bills and keeping warm, at a time when the costs of travel increase to reflect rising costs.

Notes

one COVID-19 and the Immobility Turn

1   Socio-demographic data on Portugal, including material from the 2021 census, are from the Pordata portal: www.pordata.pt/.
2   OECD, 'Receipts and expenditure', *OECD.Stat* [online], Available from: https://stats.oecd.org/Index.aspx?ThemeTreeId=10&DatasetCode=tourism_rec_exp [Accessed 10 April 2022].
3   UNWTO, 'UNWTO Tourism Recovery Tracker' [online], Available from: www.unwto.org/tourism-data/unwto-tourism-recovery-tracker [Accessed 10 April 2022].
4   European Commission, 'Erasmus+ factsheet and statistics on Erasmus+' [online], Available from: https://erasmus-plus.ec.europa.eu/resources-and-tools/statistics-and-factsheets [Accessed 10 April 2022].
5   These figures relate to enrolments made during the first semester of the academic calendar, which will include visits that were curtailed or did not actually take place during the pandemic years.
6   Pordata, 'Gross immigration rate' [online], Available from: www.pordata.pt/en/Europe/Gross+immigration+rate-1934 [Accessed 10 April 2022].

two Theorizing the Immobility Turn

1   Derived from the *The Ballad of Reading Gaol*, 'Yet each man kills the thing he loves', published in 1897.
2   It is of course possible to use 'moral economy' in an atheoretical manner and imply that there is morality in a normative sense associated with certain forms of mobility. In fact, this has already been done in regard to analytical work on pandemic era migration (see, for example, Seiger, 2021), with a focus on norms and values, and discourses, regarding what is deemed ethically acceptable behaviour. See also Fassin (2005).

three From Overtourism to Undertourism, and Back Again

1   It is also worth remarking that Portugal is an important destination for domestic tourism, including some of the sites less visited by foreign visitors (see Fonseca and Ramos, 2011).

four International Student Mobility and Immobility

[1] European Commission, 'Erasmus+ factsheet and statistics on Erasmus+' [online], Available from: https://erasmus-plus.ec.europa.eu/resources-and-tools/statistics-and-factsheets [Accessed 1 March 2022].

[2] While at the time of writing, this change has yet to be registered in official Erasmus statistics, the figures from Portuguese universities cited in Chapter 1 imply that the drop in numbers was substantial in regard to credit mobility in 2020, but degree enrolments from overseas students actually appear to have increased.

[3] The authors would like to thank the co-authors of these articles, Thais França, Daniel Malet Calvo and Leonardo Azevedo, for their invaluable contributions, including the interview material.

five Maintaining Migration during a Pandemic

[1] Three SEF officials were convicted of killing Ukrainian labour migrant Ihor Homeniuk at Lisbon airport in March 2020. The service has been threatened with extinction, but its replacement by a Portuguese Agency of Migration and Asylum has been delayed by the COVID-19 pandemic.

[2] Historically, the quality of accommodation in Portugal has been a problem for many workers, exacerbated in recent years by rampant real estate speculation, gentrification and touristification, with dramatic rises in house prices and practices such as the conversion of residential properties into short-term lets for tourists (Silva et al, 2020a, 2020b; Pinto, 2021; see also Chapter 3).

[3] Portugal's lack of popularity with workers needed in sectors like agriculture is a major concern, with Portugal only the 18th most popular country in the EU among foreigners, according to the Observatory for Migration (Observatório da Emigração), a unit within the High Commission for Migration (Alto Comissariado para as Migrações – ACM) of the Presidency of the Council of Ministers (Monteiro and Oliveira, 2021a; see also Oliveira, 2021b).

six Mobility after an Immobility Turn

[1] The decision to host Chelsea Football Club seems even more curious, given that the club's then owner, Roman Abramovich, had links with Vladimir Putin, who was later sanctioned by the EU after the invasion of Ukraine.

[2] British readers may have also noted the law-making and law-breaking of Prime Minister Boris Johnson, who was fined for having a birthday

party during lockdown and is alleged to have attended many more social events at times when such gatherings were prohibited. Likewise, the actual law enforcement body with the authority to prosecute, the Metropolitan Police in London, gained notoriety for the criminality of its police officers during the pandemic, including at least one murder.

References

Adey, P. (2006) 'If mobility is everything then it is nothing: Towards a relational politics of (im)mobilities', *Mobilities*, 1(1): 75–94.

Agasisti, T. and Soncin, M. (2021) 'Higher education in troubled times: On the impact of COVID-19 in Italy', *Studies in Higher Education*, 46(1): 86–95.

Allaste, A.-A. and Nugin, R. (2021) 'Mobility and participation: The intertwined movement of youth and ideas', in D. Cairns (ed) *The Palgrave Handbook of Youth Mobility and Educational Migration*, Basingstoke: Palgrave Macmillan, pp 185–97.

Anderson, B. (2017) 'Towards a new politics of migration?' *Ethnic and Racial Studies*, 40(9): 1527–37.

Azevedo, L., França, T. and Cairns, D. (2022) '"You're better being poor here": Migration decision-making and political and lifestyle considerations among highly qualified Brazilians in Portugal', *Revista Migraciones*, 56: 1–16.

Bauman, Z. (2000) *Liquid Modernity*, Cambridge: Polity.

Benson, M. and O'Reilly, K. (2009) 'Migration and the search for a better way of life: A critical exploration of lifestyle migration', *The Sociological Review*, 57(4): 608–25.

Benson, M. and O'Reilly, K. (2016) 'From lifestyle migration to lifestyle *in* migration: Categories, concepts and ways of thinking', *Migration Studies*, 4(1): 20–37.

Bok, D. (2009) *Universities in the Marketplace: The Commercialization of Higher Education*, Princeton, NJ: Princeton University Press.

Brooks, R. and Waters, J. (2011) *Student Mobilities, Migration and the Internationalization of Higher Education*, Basingstoke: Palgrave Macmillan.

Brooks, R. and Waters, J. (2018) *Materialities and Mobilities in Education*, Abingdon: Routledge.

Cairns, D. (2017) 'The Erasmus undergraduate exchange programme: A highly qualified success story?' *Children's Geographies*, 15(6): 728–40.

Cairns, D. (2021a) 'Migration decision-making, mobility capital and reflexive learning', in D. Cairns (ed) *The Palgrave Handbook of Youth Mobility and Educational Migration*, Basingstoke: Palgrave Macmillan, pp 25–34.

Cairns, D. (2021b) 'Mobility becoming migration: Understanding youth spatiality in the twenty-first century', in D. Cairns (ed) *The Palgrave Handbook of Youth Mobility and Educational Migration*, Basingstoke: Palgrave Macmillan, pp 17–24.

Cairns, D. and Clemente, M. (2021) 'The intermittency of youth migration', in D. Cairns (ed) *The Palgrave Handbook of Youth Mobility and Educational Migration*, Basingstoke: Palgrave Macmillan, pp 1–11.

Cairns, D., Cuzzocrea, V., Briggs, D. and Veloso, L. (2017) *The Consequences of Mobility: Reflexivity, Social Inequality and the Reproduction of Precariousness in Highly Qualified Migration*, Basingstoke: Palgrave Macmillan.

Cairns, D., Krzaklewska, E., Cuzzocrea, V. and Allaste, A.-A. (2018) *Mobility, Education and Employability in the European Union: Inside Erasmus*, Basingstoke: Palgrave Macmillan.

Cairns, D., França, T., Malet Calvo, D. and Azevedo, L. (2021a) 'An immobility turn? The Covid-19 pandemic, mobility capital and international students in Portugal', *Mobilities*, 16(6): 874–87.

Cairns, D., França, T., Malet Calvo, D. and Azevedo, L. (2021b) 'Immobility, precarity and the Covid-19 pandemic: The impact of lockdown on international students in Portugal', *Journal of Youth Studies*, 25(9): 1301–15.

Cairns, D., França, T., Malet Calvo, D. and Azevedo, L. (2021c) 'Youth migration in the age of pandemic immobility', in D. Cairns (ed) *The Palgrave Handbook of Youth Mobility and Educational Migration*, Basingstoke: Palgrave Macmillan, pp 465–75.

Capocchi, A., Vallone, C., Pierotti, M. and Amaduzzi, A. (2019) 'Overtourism: A literature review to assess implications and future perspectives', *Sustainability,* 11(12): 3303.

Carlà, A. (2022) 'Securitizing borders: The case of South Tyrol', *Nationalities Papers*, 50(1): 166–84.

Carolan, C., Davies, C.L., Crookes, P., McGhee, S. and Roxburgh, M. (2020) 'COVID 19: Disruptive impacts and transformative opportunities in undergraduate nurse education', *Nurse Education in Practice*, 46: 102807.

Carvalho, J.M. (2021) 'A imigração e a agricultura no Alentejo no século XXI', *Revista Migrações*, 17: 87–104.

Carvalho, J.M. and Duarte, M.C. (2020) 'The politicization of immigration in Portugal between 1995 and 2014: A European exception?' *Journal of Common Market Studies*, 58(6): 1469–87.

Cocola Gant, A. and Gago, A. (2021) 'Airbnb, buy-to-let investment and tourism-driven displacement: A case study in Lisbon', *Environment and Planning A: Economy and Space*, 53(7): 1671–88.

Comissão Local para a Interculturalidade (2019) *Odemira Integra+: Plano Municipal para a Integração de Migrantes 2018–2020*, Odemira: Comissão Local para a Interculturalidade.

Comissão Local para a Interculturalidade (2020) *Odemira Integra 3G: Plano Municipal para a Integração de Migrantes 2020–2022*, Odemira: Comissão Local para a Interculturalidade.

Comissão Municipal do Imigrante (2015) *Odemira Integra: Plano Municipal para a Integração dos Imigrantes 2015–2017*, Odemira: Comissão Municipal do Imigrante.

Corkill, D. and Eaton, M. (1998) 'Multicultural insertions in a small economy: Portugal's immigrant communities', *South European Society and Politics*, 3(3), 149–68.

Cresswell, T. (2006) *On the Move: Mobility in the Modern Western World*, New York: Routledge.

Cresswell, T. (2011) 'Mobilities I: Catching up', *Progress in Human Geography*, 35(4): 550–8.

Cresswell, T. (2020) 'Valuing mobility in a post COVID-19 world', *Mobilities*, 16(1): 51–65.

Cuzzocrea, V. and Cairns, D. (2020) 'Mobile moratorium? The case of young people undertaking international internships', *Mobilities*, 20(3): 416–30.

Cuzzocrea, V., Krzaklewska, E. and Cairns, D. (2021) '"There is no me, there is only us": The Erasmus bubble as a transient form of transnational collectivity', in V. Cuzzocrea, B. Gook and B. Schiermer (eds) *Forms of Collective Engagements in Youth Transition: A Global Perspective*, Leiden: Brill, pp 139–57.

Czerska-Shaw, K. and Krzaklewska, E. (2021a) 'The super-mobile student: Educational trajectories on the move and Erasmus Mundus', in D. Cairns (ed) *The Palgrave Handbook of Youth Mobility*, Basingstoke: Palgrave Macmillan, pp 231–50.

Czerska-Shaw, K. and Krzaklewska, E. (2021b) 'Uneasy belonging in the mobility capsule: Erasmus Mundus students in the European Higher Education Area', *Mobilities*, 17(3): 432–45.

Dalingwater, L., Mangrio, E., Strange, M. and Zdravkovic, S. (2022) 'Policies on marginalized migrant communities during Covid-19: Migration management prioritized over population health', *Critical Policy Studies*, https://doi.org/10.1080/19460 171.2022.2102046

de Boer, H. (2021) 'COVID-19 in Dutch higher education', *Studies in Higher Education*, 46(1): 96–106.

Earls, C.W. (2018) 'Popping the Erasmus bubble: Perceptions of intercultural awareness and competence of incoming Erasmus+ students and the preparation challenge', *Higher Education Research*, 3(3): 45–54.

Elmer, T., Mepham, K. and Stadtfeld, C. (2020) 'Students under lockdown: Comparisons of students' social networks and mental health before and during the COVID-19 crisis in Switzerland', *PLoS ONE*, 15(7): 1–22.

Engberson, F. (2018) 'Liquid migration and its consequences for local integration policies', in P. Scholten and M. van Ostaijen (eds) *Between Mobility and Migration: The Multi-level Governance of Intra-European Movement*, Rotterdam: Springer Open, pp 63–76.

Engberson, G. and Snel, E. (2013) 'Liquid migration: Dynamic and fluid patterns in post-accession migration', in B. Glorius, I. Grabowska-Lusinska and A. Rindoks (eds) *Mobility in Transition: Migration Patterns after EU Enlargement*, Amsterdam: Amsterdam University Press, pp 21–40.

Erayman, İ.O. and Çağlar, A.B. (2022) 'Hospitality in times of COVID-19: An evaluation in the context of the Baumanian concept of hospitality', *Hospitality & Society*, 12(1): 73–94.

Esteves, A., Estevens, A., Amílcar, A., McGarrigle, J., Malheiros, J., Moreno, L., Fonseca, M.L. and Pereira, S. (2017) *Condições de vida e inserção laboral de imigrantes em Portugal: Efeitos da crise de 2007–2008,* Lisbon: Observatórios das Migrações, ACM IP.

Faist, T. (2013) 'The mobility turn: A new paradigm for the social sciences?' *Ethnic and Racial Studies*, 36(11): 1637–46.

Fassin, D. (2005) 'Compassion and repression: The moral economy of immigration policies in France', *Cultural Anthropology*, 20(3): 362–87.

Favell, A. (2008) 'The new face of east–west migration in Europe', *Journal of Ethnic and Migration Studies*, 34(5): 701–16.

Feyen, B. and Krzaklewska, E. (eds) (2013) *The Erasmus Phenomenon – Symbol of a New European Generation?* Frankfurt: Peter Lang.

Fletcher, R. (2011) 'Sustaining tourism, sustaining capitalism? The tourism industry's role in global capitalist expansion', *Tourism Geographies*, 13(3): 443–61.

Fletcher, R. and Neves, K. (2012) 'Contradictions in tourism: The promise and pitfalls of ecotourism as a manifold capitalist fix', *Environment and Society*, 3(1): 60–77.

Fletcher, R., Murray Mas, I., Blanco-Romero, A. and Blázquez-Salom, M. (2019) 'Tourism and degrowth: An emerging agenda for research and praxis', *Journal of Sustainable Tourism*, 27(12): 1745–63.

Fonseca, F.P. and Ramos, R.A.R. (2011) 'Heritage tourism in peripheral areas: Development strategies and constraints', *Tourism Geographies*, 12(3): 467–93.

Fonseca, M.L., Esteves, A. and Moreno, L. (2021) 'Migration and the reconfiguration of rural places: The accommodation of difference in Odemira, Portugal', *Population, Space and Place*, 27(8): e2445.

Foucault, M. (1990) *The History of Sexuality: 1, The Will to Knowledge*, London: Penguin.

Foucault, M. (1991) *Discipline and Punish: The Birth of the Prison*, London: Penguin.

França, T. and Cairns, D. (2020) South-South student migration: Socially integrating students from Portuguese-speaking Africa at UNILAB, Brazil', *Globalization, Societies and Education*, 18(5): 578–88.

Gaitree Gowreesunkar, V. and Vo Thanh, T. (2020) 'Between overtourism and Undertourism: Impacts, implications, and probable solutions', in H. Séraphin, T. Gladkikh and T. Vo Thanh (eds) *Overtourism*, Cham: Palgrave Macmillan, pp 45–68.

González-Leonardo, M., López-Gay, A., Newsham, N., Recaño, J. and Rowe, F. (2022) 'Understanding patterns of internal migration during the COVID-19 pandemic in Spain', *Population, Space and Place*, 28(6): 1–13.

Gorjão, H.J. (2020) 'Governo regulariza todos os imigrantes que tenham pedidos pendentes no SEF', *Público*, [online] 28 March, Available from: www.publico.pt/2020/03/28/sociedade/noticia/governo-regulariza-imigrantes-pedidos-pendentes-sef-1909791 [Accessed 28 March 2022]

Green, P. (2020) Disruptions of self, place and mobility: Digital nomads in Chiang Mai, Thailand, *Mobilities*, 15(3): 431–45.

Higgins-Desbiolles, F., Carnicelli, S., Krolikowski, C., Wijesinghe, G. and Boluk, K. (2019) 'Degrowing tourism: Rethinking tourism', *Journal of Sustainable Tourism*, 27(12): 1926–44.

International Organization for Migration (2019) *Glossary on Migration*, International Migration Law, no 34, Geneva: IOM.

Iorio, J.C. (2021) 'The motivations that put Portugal back on the route of Brazilian higher education students', *Globalisation, Societies and Education*, 19(3): 326–42.

King, R. (2002) 'Towards a new map of European migration', *International Journal of Population Geography*, 8(2): 89–106.

King, R. and Raghuram, P. (2013) 'International student migration: Mapping the field and new research agendas', *Population, Space and Place*, 19(2): 127–37.

Komljenovic, J. and Robertson, S. (2016) 'The dynamics of "market-making" in higher education', *Journal of Education Policy*, 31(5): 622–36.

Koopmans, R. and Statham, P. (2000) *Challenging Immigration and Ethnic Relations Politics: Comparative European Perspectives*, Oxford: Oxford University Press.

Korstanje, M.E. and George, B. (2021) *Mobility and Globalization in the Aftermath of COVID-19: Emerging New Geographies in a Locked World*, Cham: Springer.

Lin, W. and Yeoh, B.S.A. (2020) 'Pathological (im)mobilities: Managing risk in a time of pandemics', *Mobilities*, 16(1): 96–112.

Makimoto, T. and Manners, D. (1997) *Digital Nomad*, Chichester: Wiley.

Malet Calvo, D. and Ramos, M.J. (2018) 'Suddenly last summer: How the tourist tsunami hit Lisbon', *Revista Andaluza de Anthropologóa*, 15: 47–73.

Malet Calvo, D., Cairns, D. and França, T. (2020) 'Southern Europe perspectives on international student mobility', *Portuguese Journal of Social Sciences*, 19(2/3): 129–35.

Malet Calvo, D., Cairns, D., França, T. and Azevedo, L. (2021) '"There was no freedom to leave": Global South international students in Portugal during the COVID-19 pandemic', *Policy Futures in Education*, 20(4): 382–401.

Marques, J.C., Candeias, P., Góis, P. and Peixoto, J. (2021) 'Is the segmented skill divide perspective useful in migration studies? Evidence from the Portuguese case', *Journal of International Migration and Integration*, 22: 577–98.

Mazzilli, C. (2022) '"There were many problems even before Covid." Recurrent narratives of crisis in policies for migrants' regularisation', *Journal of Ethnic and Migration Studies*, 48(19): 4754–73.

Mezzadra, S. (2001) *Diritto di Fuga: Migrazioni, Cittadinanza, Globalizzazione*, Verona: Ombre Corte.

Milano, C., Cheer, J.M. and Novelli, M. (eds) (2019) *Overtourism: Excesses, Discontents and Measures in Travel and Tourism*, New York: CAB International.

Mok, K.H., Xiong, W., Ke, G. and Cheung, J.O.W. (2021) 'Impact of COVID-19 pandemic on international higher education and student mobility: Student perspectives from mainland China and Hong Kong', *International Journal of Educational Research*, 105: 101718.

Monteiro, R. and Oliveira, C.R. (2021) *Números da Imigração em Portugal: Infografias da Imigração*, Lisbon: Observatório das Migrações.

Moscaritolo, L.B., Perozzi, B., Schreiber, B. and Luescher, T. (2022) 'The impact of COVID-19 on international student support: A global perspective', *Journal of International Students*, 12(2): 324–44.

Murphy-Lejeune, E. (2002) *Student Mobility and Narrative in Europe. The New Strangers*, London: Routledge.

Nhamo, G., Dube, K. and Chikodzi, D. (2020) *Counting the Cost of COVID-19 on the Global Tourism Industry*, Cham: Springer.

OECD (2020) *OECD Tourism Trends and Policies*, Paris: OECD.

Oliveira, C.R. (2021a) *Indicadores de Integração de Imigrantes: Relatório Estatístico Anual*, Lisbon: ACM.

Oliveira, C.R. (2021b) *Perceções e Factos da Imigração em Portugal. Infografias da Imigração*, Lisbon: Observatório das Migrações.

Peixoto, J. (2007) 'Dinâmicas e regimes migratórios: o caso das migrações internacionais em Portugal', *Análise Social*, XLII(183): 445–69.

Peixoto, J., Padilla, B., Marques, J.C. and Góis, P. (eds) (2015) *Vagas atlânticas: migrações entre Brasil e Portugal no início do século XXI*, Lisbon: Editora Mundos Sociais.

Pereira, C., Pereira, A., Budal, A., Dahal, S., Daniel-Wrabetz, J., Meshelemiah, J., Carvalho, J., Ramos, M.J., Miguel Carmo, R. and Pena Pires, R. (2021) '"If you don't migrate, you're a nobody": Migration recruitment networks and experiences of Nepalese farm workers in Portugal', *Journal of Rural Studies*, 88: 500–9.

Pham, H.H. and Ho, T.T.H. (2020) 'Toward a "new normal" with e-learning in Vietnamese higher education during the post COVID-19 pandemic', *Higher Education Research and Development*, 39(7): 1327–31.

PICUM (2020) *Non-Exhaustive Overview of European Government Measures Impacting Undocumented Migrants Taken in the Context of COVID-19*, Brussels: PICUM.

Pinto, T.C. (2021) 'Habitação', in R. Paes Mamede and P. Adão e Silva (eds) *O Estado da Nação e as Políticas Públicas 2021: Governar em Estado de Emergência*, Lisbon: IPPS-ISCTE, pp 78–82.

Pires, R.P. (2019) 'Portuguese emigration today', in C. Pereira and J. Azevedo (eds) *New and Old Routes of Portuguese Emigration: Uncertain Futures at the Periphery of Europe*, Heidelberg: Springer Verlag, pp 29–48.

Pires, R.P., Machado, F.L., Peixoto, J. and Vaz, M.J. (eds) (2010) *Portugal: Atlas das Migrações Internacionais*, Lisbon: Tinta-da-China.

Presidência do Conselho de Ministros (2019) *Resolução do Conselho de Ministros no 179/2019, de 24 de Outubro.*

SEF/GEPF (2021) *Relatório de Imigração, Fronteiras e Asilo 2020*, Barcarena, Oeiras: Serviço de Estrangeiros e Fronteiras.

Seiger, F.K. (2021) 'Migration infrastructure, moral economy, and intergenerational injustice in mother-and-child migration from the Philippines to Japan', *Mobilities*, 16(5): 707–23.

Seraphin, H. and Gowreesunkar, V. (2017) 'What marketing strategy for destinations with a negative image?' *Worldwide Hospitality and Tourism Themes*, 9(5): 496–503.

Sharma, N. (2020) *Home Rule: National Sovereignty and the Separation of Natives and Migrants*, Durham, NC: Duke University Press.

Sheller, M. and Urry, J. (2006) 'The new mobilities paradigm', *Environment and Planning A*, 38(2): 207–26.

Silva, M.C., Baptista, L.V., Ribeiro, F.B., Felizes, J. and Vasconcelos, A.M.N. (2020a) *Espaço Urbano e Habitação Básica como Primeiro Direito*, Vila Nova de Famalicão: Edições Húmus.

Silva, M.C., Rodrigues, F.M., Lopes, J.T., Cerejeira Fontes, A.J. and Morais, T. (2020b) *Por Uma Habitação Básica – Cidadania, Democracia Associativa e Metodologias Participativas*, Porto: Edições Afrontamento.

Sin, C., Tavares, O. and Neave, G. (2017) 'Student mobility in Portugal: Grappling with adversity', *Journal of Studies in International Education*, 21(2): 120–35.

Sin, C., Tavares, O. and Aguiar, J. (2022) 'COVID-19: Threat or opportunity for the Portuguese higher education's attractiveness for international students?' *Journal of Studies in International Education*, https://doi.org/10.1177/10283153221121396

Soja, E.W. (1989) *Postmodern Geographies: The Reassertion of Space in Critical Social Theory*, New York: Verso.

Srnicek, N. (2017) *Platform Capitalism*, New York: John Wiley and Sons.

Stawarz, N., Rosenbaum-Feldbrügge, M., Sander, N., Sulak, H. and Knobloch, V. (2022) 'The impact of the COVID-19 pandemic on internal migration in Germany: A descriptive analysis', *Population, Space and Place*, 28(6): e2566.

Taboadela, O., Maril, M. and Lamela, C. (2018) 'La superdiversidad migratoria en el medio rural: Odemira, Alentejo, un estudio de caso', *Finisterra – Revista Portuguesa de Geografia*, 107: 87–105.

Thompson, B.Y. (2018) 'Digital nomads: Employment in the online gig economy', *Glocalism: Journal of Culture, Politics and Innovation*, 1: 1–26.

Thompson, B.Y. (2019) 'The digital nomad lifestyle: (Remote) work/leisure balance, privilege, and constructed community', *International Journal of the Sociology of Leisure*, 2: 27–42.

Thompson, E.P. (1963) *The Making of the English Working Class*, Harmondsworth: Pelican Books.

Thompson, E.P. (1971) 'The moral economy of the English crowd in the eighteenth century', *Past and Present*, 50(1): 76–136.

Torkington, K. (2012) 'Place and lifestyle migration: The discursive construction of "glocal" place-identity', *Mobilities*, 7(1): 71–92.

UNWTO (2018) '*Overtourism'? Understanding and Managing Urban Tourism Growth Beyond Perceptions: Case Studies*, Madrid: UNWTO.

Urry, J. (1995) *Consuming Places*, Abingdon: Routledge.

Urry, J. (2000) *Sociology beyond Societies: Mobilities for the Twenty-First Century*, Abingdon: Routledge.

Urry, J. (2007) *Mobilities*, Cambridge: Polity.

Urry, J. and Larsen, J. (2011) *The Tourist Gaze: Leisure and Travel in Contemporary Societies* (3rd edn), London: Sage Publications.

Veerasamy, Y.S. and Ammigan, R. (2021) 'Reimagining the delivery of international student services during a global pandemic: A case study in the United States', *Journal of Studies in International Education*, 26(2): 145–64.

Volo, S. (2020) 'Overtourism: Definitions, enablers, impacts and managerial challenges', in H. Séraphin, T. Gladkikh and T. Vo Thanh (eds) *Overtourism*, Cham: Palgrave Macmillan, pp 11–26.

Wallis, E. (2020) 'Falling through the cracks: Undocumented workers in Portugal', *Infomigrants*, [online] 5 June, Available from: www.infomigrants.net/en/post/24566/falling-through-the-cracks-undocumented-workers-in-portugal [Accessed 12 December 2022]

Yang, B. and Huang, C. (2021) 'Turn crisis into opportunity in response to COVID-19: Experience from a Chinese university and future prospects', *Studies in Higher Education*, 46(1): 121–32.

Yang, Y., Zhang, C.X. and Rickly, J.M. (2021) 'A review of early COVID-19 research in tourism: Launching the *Annals of Tourism Research*'s curated collection on coronavirus and tourism, *Annals of Tourism Research*, 91: 103313.

Zazina, J. and Nowakowska, A. (2022) 'Is the "student city" lost? The rhythms of Lodz as a consumption-oriented student city through the COVID-19 pandemic lens', *Population, Space and Place*, https://doi.org/10.1002/psp.2607

Index

References to figures appear in *italic* type. References to endnotes show both the page number and the note number (231n3).